JUDGE ROY BEAN COUNTRY

To Karen Seidel.
who has visited the
county this book is
about.

Jack Shuler

JUDGE ROY BEAN COUNTRY

FOREWORD BY ELMER KELTON

JACK SKILES

Texas Tech University Press

This book was set in Humanist 521 and Palatino and printed on acid-free paper that meets the guidelines for permanence and durability of the Committee on Production Guidelines for Book Longevity of the Council on Library Resources. ∞
Cover photo courtesy of Western History Collections, University of Oklahoma.

Printed in the United States of America

Book and jacket design by Lisa Camp

Library of Congress Cataloging-in-Publication Data
Skiles, Jack, 1931-
        Judge Roy Bean country / Jack Skiles ; foreword by Elmer Kelton.
            p.   cm.
        Includes bibliographical references and index.
        ISBN 0-89672-374-7 (cloth : alk. paper). — ISBN 0-89672-369-0
(pbk. : alk. paper)
        1. Bean, Roy, d. 1903.   2. Langtry (Tex.)—History.   3. Langtry
Region (Tex.)—History.   4. Frontier and pioneer life—Texas—Langtry
Region.   I. Title.
    F391.S626J83   1996
    976.4'881—dc20   96-17256
                                                  CIP

97 98 99 00 01 02 03 04 05 / 9 8 7 6 5 4 3

Texas Tech University Press
Box 41037
Lubbock, Texas 79409-1037 USA
1-800-832-4042

To the memory of my parents, Guy and Vashti Skiles, and to Wilmuth, Peggy, Raymond, Russel, Diane, and Kimberly.

CONTENTS

FOREWORD

Most areas of Texas have had their folklore and history documented in row upon row of books and theses, but one area remains relatively neglected: the semi-desert region along the Pecos River. Because of its dry nature and the difficulty of wringing a living out of a land often hostile, it was one of the last parts of the state to be settled. Even today the population is sparse and for the most part relatively isolated. Some of its earliest settlers were still living until just a few years ago, and many of the region's second generation are still with us.

Though the lower Pecos has some of the state's most spectacular scenery, its gorges and deep canyons are barely accessible to the casual tourist except where the roads cross, most notably near the site of the famous old High Bridge. The average traveler hurrying through has but little idea of the rich and sometimes violent past of this harsh and forbidding land. To the stranger from greener and more benevolent climes, it appears as alien as the face of the moon.

Most of course have heard stories about Judge Roy Bean, the Law West of the Pecos, for he is one of Texas's more legendary characters, and a considerable body of myth and folklore has grown up around him. Someone— I wish I could remember who—once wrote that Americans have always had a soft spot in their hearts for the likable rogue. That has held true from Long John Silver to W. C. Fields to Bret Maverick, and it probably explains the ongoing interest in Roy Bean.

Much has been written about him—some of it true and some which should be but isn't—but the history of the harsh land in which Bean made himself at home, and of the people among whom he spent the latter years of his life, has been recorded less than that of other regions in the state.

Jack Skiles has spent his life in the Langtry country on the Rio Grande, just west of the Pecos, soaking up not only the legends but the reminiscences of men and women who were there first, who witnessed the establishment of ranching, the coming of the railroad, the growth and decline of Langtry and other towns along the lower Pecos and the Rio Grande. His account is only peripherally about the colorful Judge Roy Bean. It is devoted primarily to the land and to the hardy, iconoclastic people who challenged it . . . the cowmen and sheepherders, the railroad builders, the merchants, the laws and outlaws.

It was and is a land which seems larger than life, and the gritty folk who pioneered it also seem larger than life, eking out an elemental, often dangerous existence under conditions which most of us today would find intolerably spartan. It was a land given to furnace heat and perpetual drought, to snakes and centipedes and the stinging vinegaroon, to plants which wore an armor of thorns for self-preservation, and to independent-minded people who could be kind-hearted and open-handed, yet could quickly become as prickly as the cacti around them.

Skiles's book is a welcome addition to a small body of literature about the Pecos River country. It joins the works of Clayton W. Williams, Patrick Dearen, Paul Patterson, C. L. Sonnichsen, Alice Evans Downie, and Walter G. Downie, all of whom have touched upon facets of the region's history and folklore.

Unfortunately, much has already been lost, buried in the graves of people who saw no reason to leave a written record because they recognized little remarkable in the events they had witnessed. What we see as history today was simply everyday life to them. We are fortunate that Skiles has recorded some of their memoirs, that he has rescued part of that history so that it will not be lost to later generations who will want to know more about the heritage of the lower Pecos.

Elmer Kelton

PREFACE

Judge Roy Bean, the legendary Law West of the Pecos, is a nationally known figure in U.S. history, but fact and fiction about him have become largely indistinguishable.

Growing up in Langtry in the 1930s and 1940s, I developed an early curiosity concerning Roy Bean. I wanted to know the truth. A tree known as the hanging tree grew in the middle of the main street, but old-timers all agreed that Judge Roy Bean never did hang anyone. The old folks generally referred to Bean as "an old reprobate." The movie *The Westerner,* with likable Walter Brennan, portrayed the judge as a hero. In the movie there were cornfields all around Langtry. In actuality, only a few shrubs and cacti subsisted on the rocky hills around Langtry. I swore then that I was going to find more of the truth about Roy Bean and someday let people know the real story.

In 1963, with a secondhand tape recorder, I started interviewing everyone I heard of who had known Roy Bean. They had lived at Langtry in a different era and they had interesting tales to tell about Bean and the settlement of the area.

In 1973, I was manager of the Judge Roy Bean Visitor Center at Langtry when Arthur Newman arrived one day and said he would be one of the producers of a movie about Bean. It would star his brother Paul as Judge Bean. He said the title would be *The Life And Times Of Judge Roy Bean.* Excitedly, I told him that a movie based on the accepted facts about Roy Bean would be great because he had led an interesting, eventful life. Perhaps Newman noted my deep disappointment when he said the movie would be fiction; when the film was released, the opening credits carried the statement "Maybe this isn't the way it was . . . it's the way it should have been."

The literature about Roy Bean said that he was from Kentucky and that his parents were Francis and Anna Bean. But in courthouse records in Kentucky, I found that Francis and Anna did not have children named Roy, Samuel, and Joshua. Then I discovered that the father of the three Bean boys who all made their mark in the West was named Phantly. But Roy was the *middle* name of the fellow who became Judge Bean. Named Phantly for his father, Roy dropped his first name, which apparently has not appeared in print since 1852, when he was indicted in California for assault with intent to murder.

Historical research brings many surprises and there is still a lot I would like to know about Roy Bean and the area that I call Roy Bean's country.

ACKNOWLEDGMENTS

Roy Bean's country was and still is a tough land inhabited by tough people who will do anything to help a neighbor. I received lots of assistance in gathering material for *Judge Roy Bean Country,* and I am especially indebted to the old-timers who willingly shared their experiences and photographs and enjoyed telling me "how things used to be." They grew up without radio or television and had few books or magazines to read. They talked to each other a lot and became master storytellers, the likes of which will probably never again be known.

Those folks included my parents: Guy, a free spirit who accepted the comfort and confinement of civilization only reluctantly, and Vashti, a schoolteacher who supported and encouraged my inquisitive nature. Both offered hospitality, in their individual ways, to friend and stranger in this sparsely populated country—Dad by exchanging stories of life and adventure, Mother by providing a well-filled table and a comfortable fireside for the visitor.

These visitors included not only neighbors but also tough Texas Rangers and struggling young people who would later become professors of archaeology and geology. There were world-renowned potters, artists, writers, historians, and industrial and political leaders. Their diverse topics of discussion fascinated me and led me to become curious about many subjects. Their interest in the local lore and history also led me to a greater appreciation of it and, ultimately, to my becoming determined to tell the tale of *Judge Roy Bean Country.*

Others, whose names appear in this book, eagerly shared their stories with me and patiently answered my questions. Each will be remembered for kindnesses. Beula Burdwell Farley was a master storyteller who never forgot a date or detail. Her sister, Lillie Burdwell Shelton, frequently recalled how happy people were during hard times. Lillie's tall, quiet husband, Alfred (Big Boy) Shelton, loved horses and the open spaces.

The Shaw brothers were railroad men. Simon, Jr., knew every detail about the tracks around Langtry, and Willie remembered the funny things that happened. Rosa Babb Stapp and her sister Myrtle Babb Cash grew up ranching and stayed in the business all their lives. Myrtle wasn't afraid of anything except rattlesnakes and crossing the Pecos River Canyon in an automobile.

Cross Dodd grew up in Langtry around his father's general mercantile store, where there was always something going on. His brother-in-law, Harvey Hall, loved to tell stories, especially about his mining adventures in Mexico.

Rufus Kessler lived in Langtry only a few years, but like several other old-timers he considered the Langtry years the happiest of his life. Neal Billings, the son of an early rancher in the area, returned to Langtry and lived there as long as his health would permit. Bill McBee was an old-time cowboy who loved people and always had a funny story to tell.

How I wish there had been more time to preserve their memories! They have all passed away, but each left a unique mark on this remote country. I am glad we were able to visit and hope you enjoy their stories as much as I have.

The children of these original settlers also helped and encouraged me. Some of these include Roy (Dude) Cash, who still ranches twenty dirt-road miles north of Langtry; Myrtle Stapp Malone and her sister Dorothy Stapp Askins, active participants of the ranching industry in the area; Dorothy Billings and her husband Pete, who returned to Langtry and built a new home to enjoy retirement; Angie Winn, now living by Lake Amistad, near Del Rio; Henry Mills III, now at Del Rio but who loves the Pandale country where he ranches; Glen McBee, who appreciates a good story; and Vernon Neal Billings, the present manager of the Judge Roy Bean Visitor Center in Langtry.

Acknowledgment with appreciation also goes to the many recorders of the early history of the area. I want to thank the *San Antonio Express News* for use of material from the old *San Antonio Daily Express* and *San Antonio Weekly Express*, the *El Paso Herald Post* for material published in the *El Paso Herald*, Western Publishing Company for articles published in the *Frontier Times*, and the Texas Historical Association for information published in *Southwestern Historical Quarterly*.

I also want to express my appreciation to all the individuals and organizations who shared photographs. Although some are faded and faint, they add clarity to the story told here.

Last, but not least, I am especially thankful to my wife, Wilmuth, for her encouragement and patience concerning this project and for rescuing me from numerous computer frustrations.

JUDGE
ROY BEAN
COUNTRY

CHAPTER 1

JUDGE ROY BEAN

Putting his brand permanently on the rocky Texas country between the Pecos and the Rio Grande, Judge Roy Bean—a man with his own brand of justice and showoff ways—called himself the Law West of the Pecos. He was a tough man in a tough country, but he never had nerve enough to tell folks in Texas what his real name was.

If Roy—Old Roy, as he was known—had told those tough cowboys and hardworking, hard-drinking railroad men that his first name was Phantly, they likely would have rawhided him out of the country for having what to them would have seemed a sissified name. Although Phantly Roy Bean never revealed his full name west of the Pecos, he did get people's attention, and around 1900, when the passenger train between San Antonio and El Paso got close to Langtry, the conversations throughout the train just naturally drifted to tales about the judge.

Roy Bean had gone out west when the railroad was being built, to open a saloon and make a few fast bucks—but he had stayed and made a name for himself both in legend and history. People told about how Judge Bean had fined a corpse $40 for carrying a concealed weapon, because Bean figured that he, as much as somebody else, might as well have the dead man's money. Stories also circulated about how the judge had tried an Irish customer of Bean's Jersey Lilly saloon: the Irishman had killed one of the Chinese railroad construction men who never frequented Bean's establishment, and it seemed that the judge looked all through his law book—the only one he had—and declared, "It don't say nothing in here about it being against the law to kill a Chinaman. Case dismissed."

Just about everyone also knew that "His Honor" Roy Bean had even defied the Texas Rangers, when he helped sponsor a world heavyweight prizefight at Langtry at a time when boxing was outlawed in Texas and just about everywhere else in the United States. People were also aware of how Bean had brought law and order to the railroad construction camps and how he had befriended the poor and helped those down on their luck. When the steam locomotive stopped at the Langtry depot to take on water, all eyes turned toward the Jersey Lilly for a glimpse of this famous, self-proclaimed Law West of the Pecos. For a boy born in the hills of Kentucky, Roy Bean had come a long way.

Bean was born about one hundred miles east of Louisville in about 1835. The *Shelby Record,* a newspaper printed at Shelbyville, Kentucky has an article dated October 17, 1902 that placed Roy Bean's birthplace in Shelby County. The newspaper states that the boy's formal name was Fauntelroy (apparently a variant of Phantly Roy—which perhaps is itself a variant of Fauntleroy) Bean and that he was born west of Shelbyville, where—by 1902—there remained only a locust grove.

Census records for the state of Kentucky indicate that a man named Phantly R. Bean and his wife, Ann H., residents of Shelby County, had five children: Sarah H., James C., Joshua H., Samuel G., and Phantly Roy. Phantly—obviously the father of the man who was to be the judge—prepared the following will, dated October 12, 1835, which was recorded in the Shelby County courthouse that December:

> I Phantly R. Bean, do make and ordain this my last will and Testament. I do give and bequeath unto my wife, Ann H. Bean, all my Estate both Real and personal during her life and after death, to be Sold and Equally divided. Between my children to Wit. Sarah, James, Joshua, Samuel and Phantly, and Lastly I do hereby appoint my wife Ann H. Bean Executrix and Joshua as Executor of this my last will and Testament, without there [sic] giving Security to Court of accounting to any person whatever, and they are hereby authorised and directed to sell any lands and negroes they may think proper for the payment of my Just Debt and the settlement of my Estate and they are authorised to deed and convey my land and negroes for said purposes and further they are directed to sell any negroe when they see proper that misbehaves himself. [1]

In fact, Roy Bean's date of birth is no longer known; the census records referring to him do not agree. The Bexar County census taken July 4, 1870, listed Roy Bean as being thirty-four years old, which would indicate he was born in 1836. However, the census taken June 14, 1880, listed Roy Bean as being age forty-six, which would indicate he was born in 1834. The Val

Verde County census of June 1, 1900 showed Roy Bean having been born in Kentucky in June of 1836 and listed him as sixty-three years old. Perhaps Roy Bean did not know exactly when he was born, but it was obviously before October 12, 1835 when his father's will was made.

Roy probably left home when he was about fifteen years old. He joined his brother Samuel, who had left home in May 1845 and had hired out to drive a team of six yokes of oxen in a wagon train going from Independence, Missouri to Santa Fe, New Mexico and Chihuahua, Mexico. In 1851 the adventurous Roy Bean showed up in California, where his oldest brother, Joshua, lived. Joshua Bean earned a reputation as one of the outstanding men in southern California. He was the last alcalde of the pueblo of San Diego, and, after the city of San Diego was incorporated, Josh was elected mayor. As a civic leader, he was respected—but Joshua Bean also took good care of his own interests. According to San Diego records, it was understood before the city was incorporated that the mayor and other officials of the city would serve without pay, but just a few days after the election, the mayor and city council appropriated $6,800 for salaries for the new officials. There is little doubt that when young Roy visited Josh, he quickly began to learn some of the more sophisticated ways to feather his own nest.

Joshua was appointed major general of the state militia in 1851 and moved to San Gabriel. Josh had a general store and saloon in San Gabriel, and, a short time after Roy arrived, Josh put him to work in the establishment. Joshua also made Roy a lieutenant in the California Volunteers.

Roy lost little time in taking full advantage of his social position as the brother of a man of such prominence. He was usually seen in dashing attire and was described as "handsome as an Adonis," having a fair, rosy complexion and black, silky hair.[2]

Roy actively participated in gambling, cock fighting, horse racing, and fandangos. He was a definite success with the ladies. It was not long, however, before Roy Bean's playboy activities led to trouble: Roy engaged a man named John Collins in a duel on horseback in February 1852. The duel wound up as a social event for the people of San Diego, with a large crowd of people in attendance. Collins missed Roy Bean with two hasty shots, but Roy succeeded in shooting Collins in the leg with his first shot and blasting Collins's horse with the second.

The *San Diego Herald* of March 27, 1852 reported:

Roy Bean and John Collins were arraigned before Judge Ames yesterday on a warrant issued by Judge Witherby charging them with an assault with intent to kill. They were bound over in the sum of $1,000 each, to answer at the next term of Court of Sessions. Bean was also brought up for an assault and battery on the person of Rudolph Conrad, fined $25 and required to recognize in the sum of $100, to keep peace for 6 months.

The same newspaper reported on April 17 that the grand jury issued bills of indictment against John Collins and P. R. Bean, for assault with intent to murder and for sending and accepting a challenge. The paper also stated that "Bean having broke jail and escaped, Collins was arraigned " It is interesting to note that Bean was referred to as P. R. Bean. Roy apparently never again used the name Phantly, or even the initial P.

In November 1852, Joshua Bean was waylaid and killed one evening as he was returning home from his saloon. By this time, Roy apparently had gotten judicial matters taken care of and was again in circulation. He took over his brother's operations and was described by Major Horace Bell in *Reminiscences of a Ranger*: "I rode up to Headquarters and was met by a very handsome black bearded young man by the name of Roy Bean, brother and successor of General Josh Bean. The General had been proprietor of the Headquarters, the first grog shop of the place. Roy was dressed in an elegant Mexican costume, with a pair of revolvers in his belt, while a bowie knife was neatly sheathed in one of his red-topped boots."[3]

Roy Bean operated the Headquarters saloon for a while, but he got into a knifing scrape and had to leave California. Eventually he showed up at his brother Sam's home in Mesilla, New Mexico, completely broke and in rags.

Samuel Bean had been elected sheriff of Dona Ana County, New Mexico in 1854 and also was running a combination store, restaurant, saloon, hotel, and gambling parlor. He was described as "a big man with a big personality and the biggest voice in the territory. Some said acquired through habits of distance and bull whacking. The [drivers'] 'Gee-and-Haw' was understood by the long lines of oxen if it were loud and commanding; and stubborn mules understood emphasis. The natives [of New Mexico] called it the *'Voz del Carretero,'* the Voice of the Wagon Driver. It did carry incredible distances and could be heard all up and down Main Street."[4] Sam took Roy in, bought him new clothes, and made his younger brother presentable. In 1861,

Samuel and Roy "were dealers in merchandise and liquors and had a fine billiard table."[5]

When the Civil War gripped the land, Union forces took over New Mexico. The Bean brothers were Confederate sympathizers so Roy soon headed for Texas. San Antonio was a thoroughly Confederate town, as well as being a thriving trading center, through which goods moved to and from Mexico. Roy Bean managed to get some wagons and teams and soon was a part of that trade.

Roy Bean married Virginia Chavez in San Antonio October 28, 1866. She was the daughter of Leandro Chavez, who had a ranch about one mile south of San Antonio. The 1870 census, taken July 4 of that year, showed that Virginia was nineteen years old, so she was only fifteen or sixteen when she married Bean.

Roy and Virginia lived on the Chavez land at what later became the four-hundred block of Glenn Avenue in San Antonio, and while they lived there, the area became known as Beanville. It was there that their four children, Roy Jr., Sam, Laura, and Zulema were born. They also adopted a boy named John.

The Beans divorced after a few years. Roy moved west and remained single the rest of his life. Virginia continued to live in San Antonio; she married again and had other children.

The Bean children lived with their father at Langtry much of the time. The girls attended a convent at Galveston for a time, and both boys at one time were enrolled at St. Louis College in San Antonio. Roy Jr.'s career at St. Louis College did not last long. After a week or two he got in trouble for having a pistol tucked under his bed pillow, and he promptly headed back to Langtry. Sam, too, apparently did not stay at the school very long.[6]

Both of the Bean girls married railroad men. Laura married William J. Mellor and had three children, Mary Ruth, Charles, and Patricia. She died in Houston in 1954. Zulema married Henry Voss and died in Chicago in 1949. She had no children. Sam, who lived in the Langtry area most of his life, was killed in a street fight in Del Rio in 1908. Roy Jr. moved to New Mexico and had several children; John lived his life on ranches in the Sanderson area.

As noted earlier, while living in San Antonio, Bean got into the freighting business. A glimpse of his business was given by author Vinton Lee James, a rancher in the Uvalde area:

In the Spring of 1880, I sent word to F. A. Piper, and Company of Uvalde, to send me down some teamsters to haul my wool to San Antonio. Who should appear on the scene but Roy Bean, who afterwards became famous as the "Law West of The Pecos." He had several wagons with Mexican teamsters. Roy Bean's freight outfit to haul my wool was the sorriest I have ever beheld. The six wagons were rickety. The teams to draw same were an equal number of jackass and emaciated horses that had seen better days. The harness consisted of ropes, leather, and raw hide thongs, chains, and ill-fitted collars for the jackasses. In case of rain there was not a wagon sheet. As the weather was rainy I refused to allow him to leave. He had turned his teams into my horse pasture where the grass was fine. He stayed with me a week to allow his teams to recuperate. It surely was a comical sight to see the little jacks hitched up with the horses, with my wool aboard on the way to San Antonio.[7]

West of the Pecos

At about the same time that Roy Bean's wagons were falling apart, his marriage was also breaking up, and he began to look for a way to get away from it all. The Galveston, Harrisburg, and San Antonio Railroad was building westward from San Antonio in the spring of 1882 and was scheduled to meet the Southern Pacific, which had been progressing eastward from California. About three thousand men were building the railroad through the region where the Pecos River emptied into the Rio Grande. Roy, an experienced saloon operator, knew that all those men making good wages building the railroad would be buying lots of whiskey, so he gathered up a batch of booze and headed west to the end of the line.

Bean opened a tent saloon about three miles west of the Pecos and did a brisk business, even though there were many other saloons in the area. The railroad builders were a tough lot, and the wickedness of the railroad camps became widely known throughout Texas. In June 1882 the railroad contractors requested that Texas Rangers be sent to the construction area to maintain order. Shortly thereafter, a detachment with a Captain Oglesby in command was dispatched. Oglesby sent the following letter from Eagle Nest (later to be called Langtry) to his commanding officer, General W. H. King, on July 5, 1882:

Upon my arrival here on the 29th I proceeded to visit all the railroad camps and scout the country thoroughly. I found six of Luet. Seker's men here under Sargt. Tom Carson and feel it duty bound to say the Sargt. and men have done excellent work putting things to right and keeping the roughs strait.

There is the worst lot of roughs, gamblers, robbers, and pickpockets, collected here I ever saw, and without the immediate presents [sic] of the state troops this class would prove a great detriment towards the completion of the road. There is nothing for Rangers to do but hold this rough element in subjection and control them. The majority of the railroad camps are in Pecos County. This immediate section being two hundred miles from Stockton, the nearest jurisdiction Court of Justice and the consequent minor offenses go unpunished but I hope to remedy that in a few days by having a Magistrate appointed for this Precinct.[8]

Saloons and gambling establishments thrived at the railroad construction camps, obviously because most of the workers patronized them frequently. Apparently all of the residents of the area did not approve of the rowdy activities that went on there, as was indicated in the following letter to the editor published in the *San Antonio Daily Express:*

I wish through your column to air some abuses now existing in Pecos, Crockett, and Kinney Counties along the line of the Sunset Railway now being constructed through them, which the offices of the law in those counties either can not or, will not see. At any rate, if they do know anything of these abuses, as they should know as officers, they certainly have not taken any steps to punish the offenders. I refer to the keeping of open gambling houses every day and Sundays too, and the selling of intoxicating liquors on Sundays, for the past three months, to my knowledge, at Del Rio, Devils River Crossing, crossing of Pecos River, at Meyers Store, Eagles Nest and near the camp of several of the contractors for grading on the Sunset Railroad. It is useless for me to enumerate the many evils of whiskey selling—everyone knows them—but as everyone does not know how this affects the construction of the public

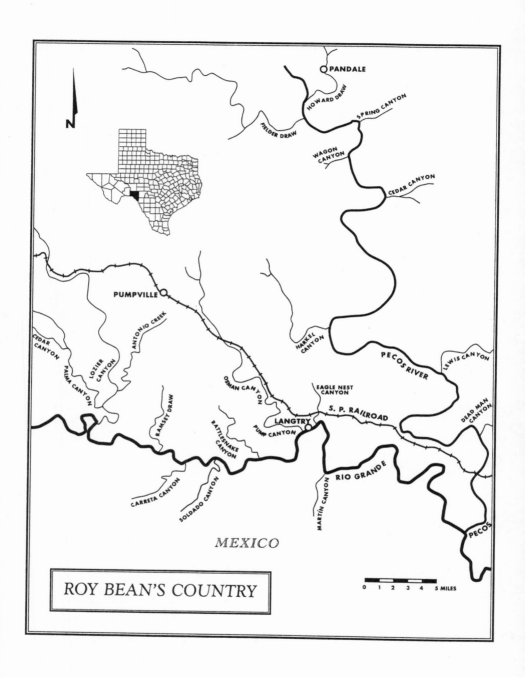

PANDALE

HOWARD DRAW

SPRING CANYON

FIELDER DRAW

WAGON CANYON

CEDAR CANYON

PUMPVILLE

HARKEL CANYON

PECOS RIVER

LEWIS CANYON

CEDAR CANYON

ANTONIO CREEK

LOZIER CANYON

PALMA CANYON

OSMAN CANYON

EAGLE NEST CANYON

S. P. RAILROAD

DEAD MAN CANYON

RAMSEY DRAW

RATTLESNAKE CANYON

LANGTRY

PUMP CANYON

CARRETA CANYON

SOLDADO CANYON

MARTIN CANYON

RIO GRANDE

PECOS

MEXICO

ROY BEAN'S COUNTRY

0 1 2 3 4 5 MILES

N

works, I will say it has been, in this case, one of the causes of increasing the price of labor to twice what much of it is worth.

A company of state rangers has been sent to Pecos County to preserve order and this they have done well, but there are no other law officers in this section of Pecos County excepting a deputy sheriff at the place called Meyers Store and I have been informed that he deals a game of monte in one of the saloons and gambling houses. There is no magistrate who is known of in that end of Pecos County closer than at Fort Stockton, the county seat, which is about 125 miles from Meyers Store. In addition to this keeping of open gambling houses and selling whiskey and other liquors on Sunday, stealing and other offenses are being committed, but as few people can spare the time and expense of going to the county seat of these counties to make complaint, then await the slowness of courts of law, the perpetrators of these offenses go scot-free. I am aware that nothing can be done to prevent the sale of intoxicating liquors on week days, but I firmly believe that if these men were vigorously prosecuted to the full extent of the law for selling intoxicating liquors on Sundays and for keeping gambling open or secret, that there would soon be very little cause for another such complaint as this and that the working men out there would have some money on hand when the railroad is completed. Do you think it could be possible that the coming election could have any effect on the county officials who have been so derelict in the performance of their duties? I know that the county commissioners of Pecos County were applied to by letter last May to appoint a magistrate for that end of the county.[9]

The outcry for a justice of the peace in that portion of Pecos County near the mouth of the Pecos River was so great that the county commissioners' court had already taken action before the letter was printed in the newspaper. On August 2, 1882, the court had met in the courthouse at Fort Stockton and passed the following resolution:

Be it remembered that on this the second day of August AD 1882, was begun and held the Commissioners Court for the County of Pecos, and the following proceedings were had:

It was ordered that Roy Bean be and is hereby appointed as Justice of the Peace for Precinct No. 6, Pecos County, Texas and the Clerk of this court is instructed to notify him of his appointment, and to give the necessary Bond and qualify within the time prescribed by Law.[10]

One of the commissioners present at the meeting in which Roy Bean was appointed justice of the peace was Cesario Torres, who owned property that would later be called Langtry. Torres's relatives would eventually experience numerous conflicts with Judge Bean.

The commissioners appointed Bean because he had been recommended to them by the Texas Rangers assigned to the area. A shady character who liked to gamble and who was often drunk in his own saloon, Bean, however, must have had some qualities that the rangers felt made him better for the job than other men in the camps. Perhaps they were aware that Bean had been on the side of law and order when he served as a lieutenant in the California Volunteers, and maybe knew that he had a brother who was a respected sheriff in New Mexico. More than likely they recognized the fact that Roy Bean was intelligent and had a commanding personality.

Roy Bean might have felt a bit strange about being on the same side as the law, but he was quick to adapt to changes: soon he was calling himself the Law West of the Pecos. From the beginning of his appointment, he was an unorthodox justice. The *San Antonio Weekly Express* of December 28, 1882 had an article describing how the new judge came into the job. The writer first sets the scene by describing Bean before his appointment:

One of the first settlers and my contemporary was 'Old Roy,' a gambler, saloon keeper, Mexican war veteran, Indian fighter, and bad man generally. He kept a saloon, but was usually so drunk and quarrelsome that people shunned his place. In one of his sober moments he realized that business was literally "going by the door," and he was seized with a sudden inspiration to brighten trade. Looking up a pair of six-shooters and a Winchester rifle, he took his position in the road, directly in front of his saloon. The first man who came along was halted at the muzzle of the Winchester and the following dialogue took place:

"Got any money, partner," asked 'Old Roy,' toying with the trigger of the Winchester.

"A little, sir," answered the stranger, with an uneasy glance at the gun. "I'm a hardworking man, and you wouldn't rob me of my little savings."

The click of the gun hammer as it flew back to full cock checked further utterance and it was some time before even 'Old Roy' could find words to speak.

"Look here, stranger," he said at last. "I'm 'Old Roy' and I'm a Gentleman. What is that you said about robbing, hey?" and he raised the gun to his shoulder.

"I beg pardon, sir," stammered the stranger, "I meant no offense."

"Oh, you didn't eh?" said 'Old Roy,' lowering the gun. "Well bein' as you're a stranger, I'll accept your apology. But you must come inside and set 'em up for the crowd."

Glad to escape so easily the frightened stranger consented to stand the treat, and between the gamblers and 'Old Roy' his pile was considerably diminished before he left the saloon. Seeing that he had a good thing, the Mexican veteran continued his system of solicitation, and so industrious was he that he soon controlled the trade of the town, and his saloon was crowded night and day. To use a favorite slang phrase, the other saloon-keepers "kicked," and petitioned for the rangers. The rangers came and the bulldozing ceased. Business again declined at 'Old Roy's' saloon and the proprietor was left to drink his own vile liquors. Before he succeeded in exhausting the supply, a commission arrived from the governor appointing the veteran a justice of peace. Money was scarce with him and he immediately convened court. A rich harvest of fines and costs was garnered by the judge the first day. He closed out the saloon and has devoted his time and talent since to expounding, upholding and explaining border jurisprudence.

Aside from his bibulous peculiarities, 'Old Roy' is generous, brave, courteous, and a keen lover of fun. He holds court anywhere and carries a pocketful of blank warrants, one of which he will fill out and sign at a minutes notice. The other morning he went down to the "bullpen" and took a look at the prisoners before court began.

"Turn those two men loose," he said, pointing out a pair of 'navvies' charged with assault and battery.

"They are charged with fighting, your honor," explained the ranger sergeant, who had them in charge.

"I don't care if they're charged with murder. Turn them loose. They are dead broke, and we don't get anything if we try 'em."

Recently his honor got very drunk and wanted to run things. "I'm the law here" he cried, jerking out his six-shooter, "and if anybody don't like it they had better hide out, for I've got my war paint on, and when 'Old Roy' gets his paint on he's hell."

The ranger sergeant expostulated with him and tried to keep him quiet.

"You have got to hold court tomorrow, judge," said the sergeant at last, with a quiet determination that meant business. "I mean to have you sober."

He seized the old veteran's pistol, called one of his men and they soon had the dispenser of frontier justice in irons. They kept him chained up until he was sober, and only released him then upon his solemnly promising to keep sober.

About five months after Bean was appointed justice of the peace, the railroad was completed and workers were laid off. Vinegaroon and the other railroad camps were abandoned. Because of an unusual abundance of water at Eagle Nest, about fifteen miles west of Vinegaroon, the railroad established a station there, naming it Langtry. Wooden houses were beginning to replace tents, so it was obviously going to be a permanent town. Roy Bean enjoyed being the Law West of the Pecos, so he moved to Langtry and vowed to stay there.

The railroad people appreciated Roy Bean because he had helped bring law and order to the railroad camps. They let him build his saloon on railroad property just behind the depot. The focal point of the community was the depot and all of the trains stopped there to take on water for their steam engines. Bean figured it was the best spot in town for his saloon. The fancy wooden saloon had a porch running all the way across its front, where the patrons could sit in the shade in the good breeze that always blew up from the river. The saloon was big enough to house a bar, a pool table, a shelf with a few groceries, a rack to hold hats and coats, and a round poker table.

Judge Roy Bean, the Law West of the Pecos, sitting on a beer keg, center, holding court on the porch of his Jersey Lilly Saloon. This building replaced Bean's larger saloon that burned in 1896 on the same site. (Photo courtesy Western History Collections, University of Oklahoma.)

Roy even built a room to serve as the office for the local Texas Ranger. The back part of the building served as living quarters—a sitting room, bedroom, kitchen, and dining room.[11]

Roy Bean never missed an opportunity to attract attention, so he had painted in big letters across the front of the saloon THE JERSEY LILLY. The name was in honor of Lillie Langtry, the English actress, famous at the time, who was born on the island of Jersey in the Channel Islands. Another, smaller sign on the front of the building proclaimed, ICE COLD BEER & LAW WEST OF THE PECOS.

Judge Bean's business flourished and in a few months he decided to open a second saloon at Sanderson. The *San Antonio Daily Express* of October 7, 1883 noted: "Roy Bean has opened a fine saloon in Sanderson, seventy miles from his other house at Langtry, where he has billiard and pool tables and the finest of liquors and cigars that A. B. Frank affords. He has just received a lot of champagne beer, which is meeting with a ready sale, being the first of its kind in the state. Passengers by rail will do well to call ahead for themselves, at either place, Langtry or Sanderson."

Bean's saloon at Sanderson did not last long. It was reported at Sanderson that Charley Wilson, who operated the Cottage Bar Saloon near the depot there, did not appreciate Bean's invasion, and one night he had an employee pour kerosene in Bean's whiskey barrel. Bean thereafter limited his saloon operations to Langtry, where he had things under control. When his appointed term as justice of the peace was up, he was elected to a full term on November 4, 1884. Bean received fifty-six votes to defeat J. S. Callahan, who got thirty-eight votes. Bean's bond as justice of the peace, in the amount of $1,000, showed H. C. Tardy, and W. F. Robinson as sureties and was approved by the Pecos County Commissioners' Court on December 10.

Bean's term as an official of Pecos County was short lived, however: on March 24, 1885 the state legislature authorized Val Verde County to be created from parts of Crockett, Kinney, and Pecos Counties. Bean was elected justice of the peace for the portion of the new county west of the Pecos in May of that year. But the change of counties apparently made little difference to the Law West of the Pecos; Bean continued his unorthodox operations as before, except that the new county seat at Del Rio was much closer than Fort Stockton.

Bean did not have a lease on the land occupied by his Jersey Lilly saloon, and in later years he was almost evicted. On November 18, 1887, N. W.

Judge Bean's notary seal, law book, pistol, and handcuffs, displayed on his poker table at the Jersey Lilly Saloon. (Photo courtesy Texas Department of Transportation, Travel and Information Division.)

Hunter, the right-of-way agent for the Galveston, Harrisburg and San Antonio Railroad (the G. H. & S. A.) sent a letter to Bean advising him that he was occupying property of the railroad and that if he did not vacate the premises within six days, legal proceedings would be instituted to remove him. Bean was not evicted, however, and on April 11, 1888 a lease agreement was entered into between the G.H. & S.A. Railway Company and Roy Bean that allowed Bean to lease the right-of-way land on which his saloon was located.[12]

Bean's large saloon, with living quarters in the back, burned in 1896. The judge immediately built a small saloon over the ashes of the larger building. His children were with him most of the time, so he decided to build a home across the street from the saloon.

Roy Bean often boasted that he was going to get Lillie Langtry to perform at Langtry, which he was claiming he had named in her honor. When folks asked what he was building across the street, Roy told them it was to be an opera house for Miss Langtry to perform in. The Bean home has always been known as the Opera House, even though the entire building was only about the size of what would be a stage in a real opera house.

Numerous stories have been told about Roy Bean and many were true, or at least based on truth, but just as many were tall tales. It was only natural that the truth would be stretched, for he was a colorful character and many of the genuine stories about the old judge were strange and interesting enough to be fiction. Well might one wonder what Roy Bean was really like.

Judge T. A. Falvey was federal judge over the district that stretched from Del Rio to El Paso at the time Roy Bean was the Law West of the Pecos. Here is Falvey's estimate of Bean, as revealed in the *El Paso Herald* in 1914:

> That man did a world of good. He was the man for the place.
> The rough community where he had settled would have tolerated
> no enforcement of the law as it was printed on the statute books.
> But they tolerated Bean, because he was both law and equity, right
> and justice. He filled a place that could not have been filled by any
> other man. He was distinctly a creation of circumstances.
>
> He was in control of the situation and his control was the only
> one possible. His decisions were not always according to the law
> and the fact, but they were accepted and that was the big point.
> Roy Bean's part in the pioneer history of west Texas cannot be writ-
> ten in a page. He was what he claimed to be: the Law West of the
> Pecos.[13]

Bean was both liked and disliked by the people who lived in Langtry. Willie Shaw, whose father was a railroad section foreman, grew up in the Langtry area during Roy Bean's time. Willie's father, Simon Shaw, Sr., helped build the railroad and was closely associated with Bean for many years. As a boy, Willie lived down the railroad track a short distance from Bean's place, and since the depot and Bean's adjacent saloon were the centers of activity in Langtry, he played there a lot, witnessing many of Bean's goings-on.

I interviewed Willie Shaw in 1966. By then, he was seventy-seven years old, but his fond memories of the judge were still vivid. Willie told me:

> I knew Roy Bean very well. He was a good friend of my father's,
> and I was around him a lot when I was a little kid. I remember old
> judge well—very well.

ROY BEAN'S OPERA HOUSE TOWN HALL AND SEAT OF JUSTICE.

Judge Bean in a cart in front of his residence, the Opera House, at Langtry. Bean told folks he built the Opera House so that actress Lillie Langtry would have a place to perform when she visited the town. (Photo courtesy of Western History Collections, University of Oklahoma.)

Old man Judge Roy Bean was a good fellow at times and then he was a mean old devil at other times. He was a rough talking fellow, but he was Law West of the Pecos and what he said went, regardless of what you had done. He was a hard old fellow, but never would let kids come inside his saloon. Every time we kids would go in Roy Bean's saloon, he would run us out. He'd say we had no damn business in there.[14]

Beula Burdwell Farley also knew Bean well. Her family lived on the Rio Grande about three miles upstream from Langtry and her father was a close friend of Bean's. Later in her childhood, she lived less than a block from the Jersey Lilly, and, like Willie Shaw, she and her family saw a lot of the judge. When I interviewed Mrs. Farley at Sanderson in 1965, she was in her seventies—but she was also noted in the area for her clear memory. She could instantly recall the exact dates of many incidents and told me:

Roy Bean was a smart ol' booger. He had his faults, but listen, he was a good man at heart. He might have been a murderer and a robber, and a thief, but he was good in his way. He was the best-hearted old fellow you ever saw. He would do anything for anybody.

Roy Bean had three houses right back of the Opera House and he had a board picket fence around the houses. Mama had all these little kids and one year the old judge told Mama that if she wanted to move to town to send the children to school he would let her live in one of the little houses and not charge her any rent. I think they normally rented for five dollars a month. There was no water and the houses had dirt floors. We lived in the first one, and it had a pretty good size room and a shed for the kitchen. Every one of the houses had a fireplace.

The other kids and I carried water from a hydrant behind the saloon. Back behind Roy Bean's saloon there was a barbed-wire fence and there was a dipping vault right there by the gate. We had to go through the gate to the hydrant, and it just ran all the time. It was the awfullest loblolly, because there were always horses there. When I would go get water, I could hear the men talking in the saloon and, oh, I was scared to death.

Roy Bean, holding his walking stick, ornately carved with images of Custer, Wild Bill Hickock, and other famous Westerners. (Photo courtesy of Western History Collections, University of Oklahoma.)

My brother, Ambrose, was big for his age, and he was a great friend of Sam Bean's. He and Sam ran around together and broke horses together, and, of course, were around Roy Bean's place a lot.

There were an awful lot of mesquite bushes around our house and around the saloon, and one evening a fellow came to our house and he asked Mama for a knife. We had a big machete to cut prickly pear and things with, so Mama loaned it to him. This fellow cut down a green mesquite and trimmed it all up. Mama said, "I can't imagine what he wants with that stick." He was a big strapping fellow—a young man. This fellow went on over toward the horse lot behind the saloon and Mama never paid any more attention to him.

That night, Ambrose came home and he was just tickled to death. He said he had saw something real funny. He said a fellow came in the saloon and he had a green walking stick—a mesquite stick—and he said the man was limping.

Mama said, "Oh, I know where that walking stick came from, because I let him have a machete to cut it with." Ambrose said he was a tall, nice-looking fellow—and badly crippled. And he said the fellow passed a hat around and all the bridge workers and everybody in the saloon put money in the hat and there was a good crowd there, too. Ambrose said that hat was just bulging with bills. Of course, those men had no place in Langtry to spend their money.

The man got the money and thanked the men, and limped on off. Ambrose and a Mexican boy followed this fellow, and he went on down the railroad track to an empty car. Of course, now the old judge didn't know the boys were following the man, and neither did the man. Anyway, there were two other fellows in this boxcar and they had a candle burning for light. He said to these other tramps, "I found a bunch of suckers. Look here what I got."

This man wasn't anymore crippled, but anyhow, Ambrose and this other boy listened to this and then they went back to the saloon and Ambrose told Judge Roy what the man had done.

So Judge Roy deputized some men—that's the way he always handled something like this—to go get this particular fellow, but not to bother the others. Judge Roy had already selected his own jury—he had to in those days. The deputies brought the fellow in directly, and set him down on the billiard table and the judge began to question him in front of the jury. They asked the man questions about it and he acknowledged to everything.

Well, they stretched him out on that billiard table and Ambrose said they cut his pants legs off, just below the knee. The judge said they would just cut his leg off and make a real cripple out of him.

The old judge had a crazy Mexican working there and he was the judge's right-hand man. He told the Mexican, "Domingo, *andale, triega la serucha,*" (hurry, bring the saw). Domingo said "Si, si" and run out the door. Directly, he came back in with an old, rusty saw. A bridge foreman was the foreman of the jury and he had one of those big old carpenter's pencils, and he marked the fellow's leg, somewhere above the ankle, where they were going to cut his leg off. He marked so hard that he nearly got the blood. The jury said, "Mark it a little higher." Then they cut the man's pants leg off a little higher and the foreman of the jury marked it again. He almost drew blood again.

Well, Mr. Dodd was almost like a chaplain around Roy Bean's saloon, because he was good on the Bible and things like that, and he was hovering over this fellow all the time this was going on. The bridge Foreman marked the man's leg two or three times and every time the jury would say, "A little bit higher." Finally, they got the leg marked pretty close to the hip and old Domingo was standing there ready to cut the leg off with that old, rusty saw whenever the judge told him to. That old Mexican was kinda crazy and he would have done it, too.

Well, they decided to all get a drink before they cut the man's leg off, so they all went over to the bar. Mr. Dodd whispers to him, "Run, run, run."

That fellow ran towards the river lickity-split and the men shot over his head and up in the air. That fellow ran right down through town towards the bluff at the river. He sure got out of there and he never was seen in Langtry anymore.

Mr. George Upshaw had a store in Langtry and he also was a rancher. He was like most of the men around Langtry in those days in that he occasionally spent some time in Roy Bean's saloon. I don't think he was a heavy drinker, but anyway, he was in Roy

W. H. Dodd, left, Langtry merchant and rancher, with Judge Bean circa 1898. (Photo courtesy of Myrtle Babb Cash.)

Bean's saloon drinking one morning with some railroad men and Roy Bean's son Sam was there, too.

It seems like Sam had a Mexican blanket and Mr. Upshaw made fun of it. Anyway, they got in such a hot argument that, and I know this is a fact, old Man Upshaw slapped Sam in the face and made his nose bleed. Directly, Mr. Upshaw picked up a Winchester. I suppose it might have been the judge's. He always kept one there. Anyway, Mr. Upshaw held the rifle and Sam's nose quit bleeding. Of course, while all of this was going on the old judge was there in the saloon watching it all.

Sam and Mr. Upshaw talked there for awhile and then they came out on the porch and he said to Sam, "I guess if I give you your gun back you will shoot me."

I don't know how long he stood there, but Mr. Upshaw handed Sam the gun and then went on down the steps leading off the porch. There were four or five steps and Mr. Upshaw walked briskly down the steps and started home. He got nearly to the railroad and Sam shot him in the back, right between the shoulder blades. Old man Upshaw turned around and he said, "Sam, don't shoot me any more. You have give me a dead shot."

Old Judge Roy had been the real cause of it. As Upshaw started off he said, "Shoot him, Sam—shoot him." After Sam shot Mr. Upshaw, the old judge said, "Shoot him again." Mrs. Upshaw and other people there said that if it hadn't of been for old Roy Bean that Sam never would have killed Mr. Upshaw. Old Judge was the cause of every bit of it.

Mrs. Upshaw and several others rushed there and Mr. Upshaw was laying on one of the tracks, and he said, "Oh, Sam shot me. I begged him not to shoot me the second time, but he did anyway." They picked Mr. Upshaw up and put him on a cot and carried him down to his house, but he died right away.

Judge Bean ate at Mrs. Dodd's boardinghouse most of the time, and one day about a year after Sam had killed Mr. Upshaw, the judge went down to Mrs. Dodd's to eat. Mrs. Upshaw was working for Mrs. Dodd as a cook and Roy Bean saw her in the kitchen and said, "Who is that cooking in there?"

Mrs. Dodd said, "Mrs. Upshaw."

Roy Bean shoved his plate back, got up and got his hat, and left. Somebody asked Bean what was the matter, and he said he was afraid that Mrs. Upshaw might try to poison him.[15]

Sam Bean was the youngest of the five Bean children and was the wildest of the bunch. He was often in trouble, but his father usually figured out some way to keep Sam cleared of the charges. After Sam killed George Upshaw, many Langtry folks figured that Roy Bean would not be able to get his son cleared of such a serious offense. But they underestimated the Law West of the Pecos. Sam Bean was acquitted at a trial held in Del Rio in 1899, but old-timers say it took most of Roy Bean's time for several months and all of his money to swing the verdict. Mrs. Farley told me:

It cost the judge an awful lot, but Sam got out of killing old man Upshaw. I think some of the men swore about Mr. Upshaw slapping Sam in the face and making his nose bleed. That was all against old man Upshaw. They didn't have any witnesses for old man Upshaw. Nobody would testify. All that bunch there testified for Sam. It cost the old man many a bottle of beer. Sam came just as clear as a whistle of that, because Judge Roy Bean had lots of friends.[16]

Mrs. Farley recalled another time that Sam Bean got into trouble:

We lived up the river from Langtry about three miles and Sam came to our house real often. He had an old black horse named Blackbird and he called the horse Old Bird. Papa had built a good horse corral—it was a round picket fence—and I remember one time Sam brought a bunch of horses and put them in our corral.
I knew there was something wrong when they started branding those horses in our corral, because they made me leave. I was just a little kid, but I knew those were strange horses. Anyway, they branded some colts and turned them out.
Well, it wasn't long until the rangers were after Sam, and it was because of those colts. Sam came to our house on Old Bird and I remember he had some perro hide-hoppers [rawhide hobbles] hanging off his saddle.

Sam Bean asked Papa to go into Langtry to see his daddy, and to bring the orders and he would be right across the river in a bunch of willows. He said his daddy would give him advice as to what to do. In fact, I think the old judge had gone to Del Rio to see what he could do to help Sam.

Papa and the old judge were good friends—just as close as could be—so Papa went into town to see Judge Roy Bean and when he came back, I remember that he told Mama to fix up some grub for Sam. He told her that the judge had said for Sam to ride, and not to show up for three months.

Mama fixed up a flour sack with some food in it and Papa started out across the river to take the word and the grub to Sam. I remember Papa's horse nearly had to swim before he got out on the other side of the river. Papa came back after a while and said that when he told Sam what the judge had said, that Sam hit his horse across the hind legs and left out.

There was a Mexican named Dortea that would bring word from Sam while he was hiding out in Mexico. This Mexican was a good friend of my brother, Ambrose, so he would bring the word to Ambrose. He liked Ambrose. He gave Ambrose a big fine hat one time. Of course, Ambrose could really talk Mexican, too. Anyway, I don't know how long it was, but the judge finally passed word to Papa to tell Sam that every thing was cleared up. Papa told Dortea to get word to Sam that he could come on back and it wasn't long until Sam came by on his way home. Getting Sam out of that scrape like to have broke the old judge. Oh, he spent a many a dollar, but he got Sam free.[17]

Roy Bean was obviously a tough old rascal, but there were lots of men west of the Pecos that were a lot tougher than Bean, although some of them were not as smart or as cunning as he was. Roy Bean knew when to be tough and he also knew when to back down from trouble.

Neal Billings, whose father, John, lived at Langtry during Roy Bean's time, told a story that showed Bean was no fool in the face of adversity, even when it involved Sam.

He told me that one day, several men were getting Langtry's race track ready for Sunday afternoon races. These were popular events that attracted people from a wide area west of the Pecos. The men had chopped out brush and weeds and were raking the track and dragging it with brush in order to get a clean racing surface. Sam Bean kept riding up and down the track, messing it up, and finally Jim Reagan, who had a reputation of being one of the toughest men along the Rio Grande, told Sam to get that horse off the track and keep it off.

Billings told me that Sam just kept racing up and down the track. Jim Reagan grabbed a stick and jumped on his horse and rode up to Sam and beat him over the head with it a few times, and finally convinced Sam that he had better stay off the track.

Sam rushed up to his father's saloon and showed Bean how Jim Reagan had bruised him, so Roy came out of the saloon with his rifle and headed for the track. A Texas Ranger standing by the depot saw that Roy was up to something, and asked where he was going with the rifle. Bean told the ranger what had happened and said he was fixing to go to the race track and kill Reagan for beating up his boy.

A freight train was stopped in front of the depot, taking on water. As Bean started to climb between the cars and proceed on foot, the ranger, who knew the judge very well, said, "I don't know whether we can get enough lumber off this freight train or not." Roy Bean stopped and turned around to face the ranger and said. "What do you want lumber off the train for?" The ranger calmly explained, "Old man John Billings went in his house down the street and got his gun, and since he is a friend of Jim Reagan's, I figure we are going to need some boards to build you a coffin." Roy Bean whirled around and took his rifle back to the saloon and stayed there.[18]

The railroad depot was the center of activity in the small town of Langtry. Cowboys and railroad men frequented the restaurant located in the north end of the depot, and all of the trains stopped at Langtry to take on water. Passenger trains came through several times a day, and those folks frequently got off the train for a few minutes to stretch or get a hard drink at the Jersey Lilly. The saloon, just behind the depot freight dock, was a busy place. It added to the excitement of the depot area.

The older kids of the community usually played around the depot and saloon unless they were swimming in the Rio Grande, or in Pump Canyon, or Mile Canyon. The kids were not allowed inside the Jersey Lilly and were frequently run out of the depot, but there were always horses, donkeys, and mules to look at. Anyway, exciting things just had a way of happening near the saloon.

Willie Shaw told me why he liked to hang out around the Jersey Lilly:

Me and Jesse Bond (we called him Cheese) were kids there at Langtry and we both hung around the old judge's saloon a lot. Roy Bean had a big bear and a big wolf that he kept there close to the saloon. He had the bear tied to a mesquite tree and just beyond the bear he had a beehive. Cheese Bond and I were just kids. I don't know how old we were then, but probably ten or eleven years old, maybe twelve. But anyhow, we were big enough that we got darned good whippings when we got home after messing with Roy Bean's bees.

You see, we went over there and neither one of us had ever seen any bees before. I went up there and those bees were coming out of a hole in the hive, so old Cheese says, "Wait a minute, let me get a stick to stop up that hole with, and we will get some honey." So he stuck a stick in the hole in the hive, and when he did the bees just swarmed out of there. They got all over me and all over him and we started to run, hollerin' and running home.

This Bond boy's father was the pumper at Langtry at that time and Papa was the section foreman. We lived pretty close together there and Mama heard us hollering and started running to us. As we came by Mrs. Bond's house, she told Mrs. Bond, "I think something has happened to them kids." Both women started running over to where we were. When they got close to us, the bees got all over them and they just had a devil of a time with those bees. They threw their aprons over their faces to hide from the bees and took off towards the house with us kids. Of course, when we got quite a ways from the saloon, the bees quit us and went back to the hive. But boy, we really got a whipping when we got home, and we never did go back to messing around with those bees.

After they took the bear and coyote away from the saloon, I did not have much business there any more. Once in a while, I would go up to the saloon to get corks, though.

In those days the beer bottles all had corks in them. Roy Bean had a big barrel just outside the back door of his saloon and when they would sweep out the saloon, they would throw the corks in the barrel. I don't know why they kept those corks, but anyway, us kids would get two sacks and fill them with corks and tie the ends of them and put a rope between them and make water wings out of them. They sure were a lot of fun to swim with.[19]

Most of the men of the town also spent a lot of time around the depot and saloon, because there was always something to do or someone to talk to. When things got too dull around the Jersey Lilly, Bean, with his good sense of humor, could usually figure out something that would be exciting and good for a few laughs. Beula Burdwell Farley told me of one such incident:

They had a work train at Langtry, and old Moose Collins was the conductor. He came in and reported to old Judge Roy that somebody had stolen a six-shooter and some groceries out of the caboose. Well, they picked up a young man for stealing the stuff, and he was a New Yorker—a nice looking kid. He acknowledged to all of it, so Roy Bean said, "Well, there isn't nothing bad about stealing the food if you were hungry, but why did you take the six-shooter?"

The boy was pretty scared and couldn't give a good enough explanation, so judge and his appointed jury decided to hang him.

There was a train standing on the track, so they decided to hang the boy from one of the cars. Somebody went around to the other side of the railroad car a'horseback and they *dar le vueltad* [wrapped it around the saddle horn] the end of the rope to the saddle and ran the other end through the brake wheel on top of the car and down to the boy. They tied the rope to the boy's neck and were going to scare him real good with their joke.

But you know, that horse got scared and jumped a little, and he pulled that boy way up on the car before they could stop that horse. Of course, he did not stay too long, because somebody cut him loose. That boy went down the track just a'flying and the men were hollering and whooping at him.

The men had a lot of fun out of it, but it almost developed into a tragedy.[20]

Judge Roy Bean on a hill overlooking Langtry. At left is his original Jersey Lilly that burned in 1896. To the right of it are the Langtry depot, the Fielder home, the Torres home, and the water tank used to supply steam locomotives. (Photo courtesy of Texas Department of Transportation, Travel and Information Division.)

Judge Roy Bean might have been mean and cruel, but his kindness to children endeared him to the hearts of the young. He was very generous to the children of the Langtry community, but he also respected the fact that young people had no business in a saloon, as Cross Dodd remembered. Dodd was the oldest son of William Henry Dodd, who moved to Langtry in 1896 to operate a grocery store and became postmaster. Educated in England and respected in Langtry for his business abilities and better-than-average schooling, W. H. Dodd was close friends with Bean and some of Cross Dodd's earliest memories involved the judge. When I interviewed him in 1963 in Austin he recalled:

> My mother had a boardinghouse and Roy Bean ate there all the time. When I knew him, the old gentleman always had a beard. He was heavyset and was about like any other man in town. He was pretty jovial and was a likable old fellow. We did not think of him as rough, or mean, or out of the ordinary.
>
> He had a saloon across the track there, and if youngsters gathered up beer bottles and took them up there he would pay you for them. I guess he shipped the empties back. He would not let kids go in the saloon, though. I do not remember ever being in the saloon at all. He would always come out on the front porch to buy the bottles.[21]

Rosa Babb Stapp, the daughter of a pioneer Langtry family, also had fond memories of Bean. The family owned a large ranch north of Langtry, but the children and their mother stayed in town during the winter so the kids could go to school. They rented a house—made of railroad ties—a short distance from Bean's saloon, down Torres Avenue. Mrs Stapp remembered:

> We moved in to Langtry in 1902 and the first Christmas we were in Langtry, Old Judge Roy Bean asked Mr. Dodd to give him the names of all us kids, and there was a Christmas present on the tree from Roy Bean for every one of us kids, except me. Mr. Dodd didn't know us very well, and he just didn't give Roy Bean my name.[22]

Bean was not only good to the children of Langtry, but he also took a strong interest in their schooling. In 1901, Bean was serving as a school trustee and on September 9 of that year he signed a contract hiring Miss Winnie Elkins as a teacher in the Langtry school. Miss Elkins was to be paid a salary of $35 per month and her salary was to be paid largely from a tuition charge of $1 per month for pupils of scholastic age and $1.50 for students over scholastic age.

Roy Bean also saw to it that there was an adequate stack of heating wood behind the school house each winter and he made frequent visits to the school to see how things were going. He was interested in the children, but it was reported that there were also times when he was interested in the school marms. However, at least one Langtry teacher was not at all interested in Roy Bean. She even refused to eat at the same table with him at Mrs. Dodd's rooming house because he was so filthy and his table manners were so repulsive.

Prize Fight: Bean's Greatest Claim to Fame

Judge Roy Bean was a good showman and he made the most of every opportunity to attract attention to himself. His biggest show and greatest claim to fame came from his part in staging the championship boxing match between Robert Fitzsimmons and Peter Maher in 1896.

Prizefighting had been outlawed in most of the states but was legal in Texas, so Dallas promoter Dan Stuart arranged for world heavyweight champion James J. Corbett—Gentleman Jim Corbett—to fight Bob Fitzsimmons, an Australian who was considered by many as the number one contender for the title. Texas governor Charles Culberson, not wanting his state to go against popular national sentiment, called a special session of the legislature, which passed the Texas Act of 1895, banning prizefights in Texas.

Promoter Stuart was determined to sponsor a fight, so he made arrangements for the contest to be held October 31, 1895 at Hot Springs, Arkansas. However, the Arkansas governor sent his state militia to Hot Springs to prevent the fight. Gentleman Jim became disgusted with the entire process; he then announced that he was retiring from the ring.

Peter Maher, the champion of Ireland, was considered a strong challenger for the championship, so Stuart arranged for Fitzsimmons and Maher to meet for the world title. On January 10, 1896, Dan Stuart announced in El Paso that the fight would be held in the El Paso area. Fitzsimmons soon arrived in

El Paso to begin training, and Maher opened a training facility in Las Cruces, New Mexico. When Stuart opened his headquarters in Juárez, Mexico—across the river from El Paso—it was generally believed that the fight would be held in that city.

On January 14, 1896, Stuart announced that the championship fight would be held on February 14 and that tickets would go on sale the following day. He did not specify, however, where the fight would be held. The governor of the Mexican state of Chihuahua soon came to Juárez and announced that he would not allow the fight to be held in his state. It was then generally assumed that the long awaited fight would be held in New Mexico Territory. However, there was strong interest in the fight all over the United States and so much pressure to outlaw boxing universally that the U.S. Congress swiftly passed a bill outlawing prizefights in territories. By this time, although there had still been no announcement as to where the fight would be held, fight fans were gathering at El Paso. Dan Stuart had guaranteed a $10,000 purse and his contract provided that he would forfeit $5,000 to each fighter if he did not provide a battleground. As the anxious fight fans milled around in El Paso, it appeared certain that Stuart was going to lose his money. Additional *rurales* (Mexican federal police) had been sent to Juárez to keep the fighters out of Mexico and twenty-six Texas Rangers—a force of unheard-of size—were in El Paso to keep the fight from being held on Texas soil.

On the morning of February 14, Stuart announced that Maher had eye trouble and that the fight would have to be postponed a few days. Six days later, the fight fans were told that a special train would leave El Paso that night to take them to the fight, which would be held the next day. The rail tickets cost $12 and showed the destination to be Langtry. The tickets to the fight cost $20.

The fans boarded the train about eleven o'clock that night. It was not a special train, as had been announced, but about four cars had been added to the regular eastbound passenger train. In addition to the fight fans, several Texas Rangers, headed by a Captain Mabry, were on board, with orders to see that the fight was not held in Texas. Twenty deputy U.S. marshals from New Mexico Territory, under the command of George Curry, were also aboard the train in case the rangers needed help.[23] It is generally believed that Stuart had talked to Roy Bean sometime in January about the possibility of the fight being held in Mexico, just across the muddy Rio Grande from the town of Langtry. The Texas Rangers apparently learned where the fight

Scene at the Fitzsimmons-Maher world heavyweight championship fight, held February 22, 1896, in Mexico opposite the mouth of Eagle Nest Canyon. The screens did not work: many fans watched from surrounding bluffs. (Photo courtesy of Western History Collections, University of Oklahoma.)

Temporary bridge laid across the Rio Grande at Eagle Nest Crossing for the Fitzsimmons-Maher fight. The bridge was removed shortly after the fight. (Photo courtesy of Western History Collections, University of Oklahoma.)

would be when some of them followed a railroad car, bearing material for the ring, to Langtry. They telegraphed the sheriff of Val Verde County, advising him of the situation, and a deputy was sent to Langtry. Judge Bean quickly bluffed the lawmen. He got them so confused that they dispatched a telegram to Governor Culberson on the morning of February 21, 1896: "Prize fight takes place across river. Whose jurisdiction are we under, yourself or Judge Roy Bean. Await your instructions. I. G. Reagan, Deputy Sheriff."[24] A copy of Culberson's reply is not available, but the governor was probably not very happy with the Law West of the Pecos, and he obviously meant for his Texas Rangers to take charge of the situation.

The train bearing the two fighters, correspondents, lawmen, and fight fans arrived at Langtry at about 3:30 on the afternoon of February 22. The group climbed off the train and immediately swarmed around the Jersey Lilly.

Business had never been so good at Bean's saloon, but it was getting late and Dan Stuart insisted that the fight get under way as soon as possible.

The weather had turned cold and a drizzling rain had set in as Judge Bean led the fighters and crowd toward the Rio Grande. The crowd of visitors and local citizens walked down the main street of Langtry with cowboys from local ranches on horseback. They followed the wagon trail down the low limestone bluff to the river and then proceeded downstream to a footbridge that had been erected for the occasion at the famous Eagle Nest Crossing.

The large force of lawmen that had assembled at Langtry to prevent a prizefight on Texas soil had no authority in Mexico, so they stayed on the Texas side of the Rio Grande, where they could watch the fight from the top of a bluff. There were no Mexican officials on hand to stop the fight: Mexican authorities were not aware that such activities were about to take place in their country, in that desolate section of the State of Coahuila.

The pugilists and fans crossed the bridge and walked about one hundred yards downstream to the ring that had been hastily erected on a sandbar, just opposite the mouth of Eagle Nest Canyon. The ring, built of white pine, was covered with canvas and was four feet high. A circus canvas, two hundred feet in circumference and sixteen feet high, circled the ring, supposedly to prevent people who had not purchased tickets from watching the fight; however, the barrier was completely useless, because fans who had not wanted to pay for admission could watch the fight from bluffs on either side of the river: no world heavyweight championship fight had ever been held in a more scenic setting: all but 182 of the fans chose to·watch the fight from the rural balcony.

The fight had to wait while a work crew drove the ring stakes and set the ropes, and there was additional delay while a kinescope (predecessor of the movie camera) was being readied. Almost $10,000 had been expended by Eastern businessmen in an attempt to record the fight with the kinescope, but as it turned out, the effort was in vain because of the dark conditions caused by the cloudy, dreary weather.

Fitzsimmons and Maher had dressed on the train, so they had only to remove their overcoats, caps, and trousers before hopping into the ring. The two great pugilists stepped to the center of the ring to shake hands and listen as referee George Siler gave a brief warning that they obey the rules of the game. Siler produced five-ounce gloves and they were fitted to the hands of

Fitzsimmons and Maher. Timekeeper Lou Housman struck the gong and the fight was on.

Maher drew blood from Fitzsimmons's lip, but after only a minute and thirty seconds of lively fighting, Fitzsimmons won the match with a right-hand punch to Maher's jaw that dropped the Irish champion to the canvas. Fitzsimmons fans cheered as Maher was counted out and carried to his corner. It was several minutes before Maher realized what had happened, but he regained his feet to shake hands with the champion. Fitzsimmons received the *Police Gazette* diamond belt representing the championship of the world and the promise that he would receive the $10,000 that had been left safely in El Paso.

The crowd hastily retreated through the drizzle to Roy Bean's saloon for more drinks, and just before dark the westbound passenger train chugged out of Langtry, headed for El Paso.

After the Fight

The prizefight had not lasted long, but it brought international fame to Judge Roy Bean and the little town of Langtry. From that day on, people visited Langtry to see the legendary judge, and more and more stories circulated about him. Accounts of Bean's antics frequently appeared in newspapers throughout Texas. An example from the *Alpine Avalanche* of March 8, 1901, reprinted from the *Hondo Herald*, ran:

> Charles Sheidemantel, who has just returned from a trip out West, tells a new story of Judge Roy Bean, the unique "Law West of the Pecos."
>
> A few days ago the Sunset Limited was delayed at Langtry for some ten or fifteen minutes on account of a hot box [a hot wheel bearing]. Some of the lady tourists had desire to feel terra firma under their feet, and in strolling along, discovered Judge Roy Bean's establishment, they resolved to inspect it, and as it were got a glimpse of the home life of the man whose fame has spread throughout the United States.
>
> Cautiously approaching the front entrance they peeped in. An exclamation—whether of admiration or astonishment is not related—burst from their lips and one of the ladies remarked, "I wonder where the proprietor is."

At this the Judge's deep voice was heard inside: "By G—, I am the proprietor, and emerging from the semi-darkness he sized up his visitors and added: "Look here, whichever one of you is Mrs. Nation, I want you to understand that your hatchet racket don't go here. I am the law west of the Pecos, and she's going to be enforced if you cut any capers around here."

Allie Berry taught school at the neighboring community of Pumpville from 1901 to 1903 and she provided me with information about Bean and travelers who stopped at his saloon. In an interview, she painted a graphic word-picture of what Bean looked like:

Sometimes Judge Roy Bean would come up to Pumpville. He always rode a'horseback. He would come in the house and visit, but he never would take his hat off. He would come in and sit down at the table, but he never would take his hat off. He wore those old cowboy chaps or leggins, and he would take them off before he came in the house, but he never would take his hat off. He would always apologize to Mrs. Shaw and Mr. Shaw would say, "Anna me darlin', she's the sweetest woman in the world. She don't care, she won't get mad at you cause you don't take your hat off."

Roy Bean always wore a white shirt and he always wore a duckin' tan-colored jacket. He nearly always had a big handkerchief around his neck but I saw him once in a while without it. He was the kind of a man that if you owed him a nickel, he wanted it. And if he owed you a nickel, he was going to pay it. He was honest about everything.

He had a saloon at Langtry, and the train went right by it. The passenger train always stopped there about twenty or thirty minutes. One day I happened to be on the train, coming home from seeing my oldest sister, and there were a couple of men on the train talking about Roy Bean. They were kinda smart-aleck-acting fellows and they heard a lot about Judge Roy Bean, and they heard nobody could ever get by with doing anything to him. They were determined they were going to do something.

When the train stopped at Langtry, a lot of the men would always get off and go over to Judge Bean's to get a drink or two.

These two men decided they were going to beat him out of their drinks. They weren't going to pay for them. Well, they waited till the very last minute and by the time the conductor had hollered "All aboard" and everybody came out to get on the train, these fellows ran up to Judge Bean's bar and ordered a quart of whiskey. The judge handed them their whiskey and looked up and saw that one of them had a twenty dollar bill and he said, "Just a minute, and I'll get the change" [the man keeping the twenty dollars in his hand] Well, the men grabbed their bottle of whiskey and went and got on the train.

About six months or a year later, I happened to be on the train again, coming back from seeing my sister again, and these same men were on there. These fellers were salesmen of some kind—drummers—and they were laughing and talking about what they was gonna do. They were gonna get some whiskey and not pay for it, using a twenty-dollar gold piece. The men got off the train and went in the saloon and waited until the last minute to order their whiskey. They ordered the whiskey and Roy Bean said "Give me the money," so they gave him the twenty-dollar gold piece. About that time, the conductor hollered "All aboard," so they wanted their change back. Roy Bean said, "Go on, I remember you from before, so I got no change. You better go on and get on your train. If you don't they will go off and leave you."

The men had to catch the train, so they lost their twenty-dollar gold piece, but they did get to keep the whiskey.[25]

Judge Bean was growing old, but he was still the Law West of the Pecos. He was elected justice of the peace for Val Verde County precinct number 5 on November 4, 1902. Then on March 15, 1903, the following letter was written by Dr. H. B. Ross to his fiancée, Miss Dade Wilkinson, of Temple, Texas:

I came up here this afternoon to see Judge Roy Bean who is desperately sick—will take him to Del Rio on the morning's train if he is still alive when it comes. I came up to see him last night but went back to Del Rio this morning and made my calls there in time to come back on this afternoon's train. Am writing you now instead of waiting until morning because in the morning will probably not have time before train leaves . . . .

Judge Roy's heart is growing weaker—have just given him a hypodermic of strychnine. He has certainly lived a stormy life.

The next day, Ross added: "Judge Bean passed into the hereafter this AM at about three o'clock," and the next morning, under March 16 datelines, newspapers throughout Texas carried the story. One clipping, from an unidentified newspaper, reads:

Judge Roy Bean, better known under the title of "Law West of the Pecos," died at 3 o'clock this morning.

Judge Bean was apparently well Saturday morning when he called to one of his hands to come to his place, claiming he was not feeling well. Toward 3 o'clock in the afternoon he was found by some of his friends acting strangely in his saloon and was asked what he was doing. He could not explain, as he was unable to talk. He was immediately put to bed and the doctor telegraphed for, but when he arrived and examined the patient, he said there was no hope. His children, although hard to locate, were notified by wire, but only one—his son, Sam, who was out seventy miles in the country—succeeded in arriving before his father died, and took the remains on this morning's train to Del Rio for burial.

Judge Bean, who was about 68 years old at the time of his death, was born in Kentucky and came to Texas a young man, after taking a trip to California. Judge Bean married about forty years ago at San Antonio to Miss Chavez, daughter of a well respected Spanish settler of that place, who survives him and still resides in that city. Judge Bean is survived by four children, Roy Jr., who is married and lives at present in New Mexico; Mrs. Laura Mellon of Algiers, La.; Mrs. Zulema Voss of Richmond, Texas; and Sam who still lived with his father. Judge Roy Bean located at this place in 1883 and ran a beer saloon ever since; he was justice of the peace of precinct No. 5 of Val Verde County since 1884, and with the exception of four years, when he was defeated by J. P. Torres, he has held the office till the time of his death.

Judge Roy Bean and his children. From left: Zulema, Roy Jr., Judge Bean, Sam, and Laura. (Photo courtesy of Western History Collections, University of Oklahoma.)

Roy Bean was buried in Del Rio's Westlawn Cemetery, March 17, 1903. His passing was symbolic of the passing of an era in the country west of the Pecos.

CHAPTER 2

EXPLORERS AND
INDIAN FIGHTERS

Judge Roy Bean, self-proclaimed as the Law West of the Pecos, is generally credited with taming the area just west of the Pecos River. He had a strong impact on the region, but his influence came only after earlier people had learned to live in that harsh environment. The region's story—in particular, the tale of the earlier days—throws light on Bean's own saga. And as the story unfolds, we shall come across Bean himself, as remembered by people of the locality.

The lower trans-Pecos is a region of steep, rocky hills drained by arroyos that converge to form deep, rocky canyons that cut through massive limestone. These canyons empty into the gorges formed by the Pecos and the Rio Grande. The rough country is made even more harsh by scant rainfall, frequent droughts, and daytime summer temperatures that for weeks on end frequently exceed one hundred degrees. The average rainfall in Roy Bean country is about fourteen inches, but that figure tells only part of the story. Some years, only three or four inches of rain falls; conversely, in June 1954 much of the region was inundated with rain, receiving more than twenty-four inches in one night.

When humans first entered the region, more than twelve thousand years ago, the climate was more hospitable: dense piñon pine forest covered much of the area. The first inhabitants probably followed the Pecos River to its confluence with the Rio Grande. Water in the two rivers and abundant vegetation along their flood plains attracted a variety of animals and provided sustenance to the first people who ventured along the waterways. Now-extinct animals that once occupied the region include horse, camel, mammoth, saber-toothed cat, small antelope, and large bison.

Open-faced caves or shelters abounded in the limestone cliffs along the rivers and canyons that branched out from them. Abundant food, water, and shelter provided for the basic needs of these people and sustained them for thousands of years. Archeological excavations at Bonfire Shelter near Langtry reveal that Paleo-Indians drove herds of buffalo over the cliff into Eagle Nest Canyon for thousands of years. Such massive slaughters ensured early residents of the canyon a supply of dried meat for several months.

By 5,500 BC, the climate had become drier. Piñon pine began to be replaced by juniper, oak, hackberry, and mesquite, but the residents of the area adapted, learning to utilize desert-type plants. They baked and ate the hearts of sotol plants and used the long leaves of the sotol to weave mats and baskets. Agave lechuguilla was used to make string, nets, rope, and sandals, and the seeds of most of the plants were ground for food. People living in the rock shelters also ate the leaves and fruit of prickly-pear, as well as wood rats, pack rats, jackrabbits, cottontails, raccoons, lizards, snakes, birds, insect larvae, beetles, grasshoppers, and fish, as determined by pollen analysis of coprolites.

The Pecos River People, residents of the rock shelters, used flint to make knives and scrapers, spear points and dart points. They did not have bows but used the atlatl (a stick that served as an extension of the arm) to propel their arrows. Arrow shafts were made of straight river-cane. They drew intricate pictographs of shamans, deer, panthers, and other images on the walls of many of the rock shelters, and they drew designs of a completely different type on smooth, stream-worn pebbles.

People inhabited the rock shelters for thousands of years, but by about 800 AD the caves were little used. The first Spanish explorers of the region encountered nomadic hunters; later these nomads were succeeded by Comanches hunting buffalo or passing through on raiding expeditions.

Historians generally agree that the first white man to see the country between the Pecos and the Rio Grande was the Spanish explorer Cabeza de Vaca, who in 1535—shipwrecked and separated from his group—wandered across southern Texas and up the Pecos River, probably to a point near the present town of Sheffield, and then across the trans-Pecos country to the mouth of the Rio Conchos, opposite the present town of Presidio.

The next European to venture into the trans-Pecos region was Antonio de Espejo, a wealthy Mexican adventurer whose organized expedition reached the junction of the Rio Grande and the Conchos in 1583. Espejo referred to the Rio Grande as the Guadalquivir River. He traveled upstream to near present-day Santa Fe, New Mexico. From that point, Espejo followed the Pecos River down to the vicinity of present-day Fort Stockton, before returning to the confluence of the Conchos and the Rio Grande. His name for the Pecos was El Rio de los Vacas (River of the Cows), because of the buffalo he found there.

Espejo's entry into the area north of the Rio Grande served as a stimulus to other explorers. Gaspar Castaño de Sosa, the lieutenant governor of the State of Nueva Leon, outfitted an expedition and left Almaden (now Monclova) July 27, 1590. His expedition to this new frontier consisted of more than 170 men, women, and children, a long supply train, and two brass, field-artillery pieces. Castaño reached the Rio Grande, which he called the Rio Bravo, September 9. The party camped there, awaiting messengers sent back to the viceroy, while advance parties went in search of the Pecos River, which they called Rio Salado (Salt River). On October 2, 1590 the members of the expedition left their camp, which was apparently near the present city of Del Rio, and traveled to what they called the Rio de las Lajas (River of the Rocks), which was probably Devils River. They crossed the river with some difficulty and two days later set out in search of the Rio Salado.

On October 6 they camped for the night at a place where much water was to be found and there were some little oaks. The next day they again set out to look for the Rio Salado, sending four scouts ahead to locate the river. The scouts located the river but reported that it would be very difficult to reach because of the roughness of the country. Another party, sent out to find a better route to the Rio Salado, came back with the dismal news that it would be impossible for the main expedition to reach the river. Castaño, determined to reach the Rio Salado, started the slow-moving expedition in a northwesterly direction and again sent out scouts to search for a suitable crossing of the river.

An advance party headed by Captain Cristobal de Heredia again located the Rio Salado, on October 7, but this group, too, reported that it would be impossible for the main party to reach the river: the river flowed through a deep canyon and, although there were a few places where horses could work their way to the water, no places had been found where the supply train could make the crossing.

The main body of the expedition continued moving northwest, camping when they could at small water holes. By October 13 they had reached some plains—probably about twenty miles northwest of present-day Comstock—and camped without water, with their scouts still reporting that the country along the Pecos was too rough for the main group to enter. A heavy rain at their dry camp encouraged the expedition members, for they felt that it was the will of God, who would continue to provide for them. The group proceeded slowly toward the northwest, and on the 16th rain again fell.

On October 18 scouts were again sent out to find a place to cross the Salado, but they could not even find the river. Some members of the expedition thought that the river had dried up and others suspected that it made a big bend to the west. Discouragement mounted as it became difficult to find enough water to sustain 170 people and their stock. De Sosa sent out six men on the 20th and told them not to return until they had again located the elusive river. On the 22nd, an abundance of water was found and on the 23rd a scout returned to report that the river had again been located and that the hills and mountains came to an end about ten miles to the west.[1]

It took Castaño twenty-three days to penetrate the bastion of the lower Pecos River. His expedition followed the east bank of the Pecos into New Mexico to continue his explorations, but nowhere did he find such difficult terrain as along the lower fifty miles of the river. De Sosa was among the first of a long line of explorers and settlers who found the lower Pecos to be an almost impenetrable barrier.

Spanish exploration continued throughout the northern frontier that would be called Texas, and by 1729 the only major portion of that frontier that had not been explored by the Spaniards was the area along the Rio Grande from San Juan Bautista to La Junta, at the juncture of the Rio Grande and Concho rivers. It was apparent to the Spaniards that this area needed more exploration. Moreover, they felt that they should punish area Indians who had conducted raids against Spaniards and Christianized Indians south of the Rio Grande.

In 1729, the governors of Coahuila and Nueva Viscaya fitted out an expedition under Captain José de Berroterán of San Juan Bautista to explore the region and search for hostile Indians. Other commanders of the expedition were Captain Múzquiz of Rio Grande del Norte and Captain Leysola of San Pedro del Callo.

Berroterán's expedition, consisting of eighty-eight soldiers and forty-six friendly Indians, set out for the unexplored territory on March 28, 1729. They traveled from San Juan Bautista up the south bank of the Rio Grande, exploring the tributaries and looking for hostile Indians. It was their opinion that the marauding Indians had their headquarters along the Las Vacas, which enters the Rio Grande from Mexico at present-day Ciudad Acuna. After failing to find Indians on the Las Vacas, the soldiers proceeded up the Rio Grande to a point near where Langtry is today, and crossed to the north side of the river. The only thing recorded concerning this crossing of the Rio Grande was that there was grass for the horses, the horses could be watered in the river, and the country was not so rough as that already covered.

The Berroterán expedition continued up the north bank of the Rio Grande until their scouts reported that the river ran through a deep canyon. It was impossible to follow the river further, due to the extreme roughness of the mountains on either side. Thwarted by the terrain, the group returned to San Juan Bautista.[2]

The Indians from the north continued to harass the Spanish and their Christian Indians, and the Spaniards felt an urgent need to establish a fort between La Junta and San Juan Bautista. Another expedition was organized in 1735 to explore both banks of the Rio Grande north of San Juan Bautista and determine a suitable location for the establishment of a presidio, or fort, to be called Presidio del Sacramento. The presidio was to be located in a position that would deter Indians traveling into the area south of the Rio Grande.

The expedition, under the command of Captain Joseph Múzquiz, set out from Monclova with twenty soldiers and their guides and servants. They obtained additional soldiers and Indian auxiliaries at San Juan Bautista and proceeded up the south bank of the Rio Grande to the San Diego River, about fourteen miles south of the Las Vacas. From this camp, Captain Miguel de la Garza Falcón, son of the governor of Coahuila, proceeded to explore the country farther north. Upon reaching the Las Vacas, he found extensive evidence of Indian habitation and decided the site would be an excellent location for the proposed presidio.

On January 5, 1736 Garza Falcón crossed to the north bank of the Rio Grande in the vicinity of Devils River at a place he called Barvacoas. He then marched on to the Pecos, which he apparently crossed near its confluence with the Rio Grande, and proceeded to explore the trans-Pecos region. The expedition apparently passed through the Langtry area and continued west-ward, but on January 6 a norther had brought cold weather, accompanied by snow. Some of the captain's horses had died along the way, and as the party pressed farther westward through the rocky country, many of their mounts became tender footed. Garza Falcón decided on January 8, 1736, that the rough country west of the Pecos was not satisfactory for the establishment of a presidio, so he turned around and proceeded back over the route by which he had come. Upon his return to his father's camp, he found that a site on the San Diego River had already been chosen for Presidio del Sacramento.

By the middle of the eighteenth century, the Spaniards had learned enough about the region immediately west of the Pecos River to know that it was too rough to be of interest to them. They apparently felt that the region was not worth the effort that it would take to develop it.

Indians were about the only people in the lower trans-Pecos region for the next hundred years. Texas became a U.S. state in 1846. Two years later, the Treaty of Guadalupe Hidalgo established the Rio Grande as the boundary of Texas and stimulated U.S. exploration into the country west of the Pecos. Also by 1848, settlers had begun establishing homesteads in the Presidio and Fort Davis areas, but were still reluctant to attempt eking out a living in the country closer to the confluence of the Pecos and Rio Grande.

During the summer of 1848, an expedition financed by San Antonio businessmen and headed by John Coffee (Jack) Hays set out to find a practical trade route connecting San Antonio to El Paso del Norte, and Chihuahua. The group traveled a circuitous route to San Felipe Springs, crossed the Devils River (and probably were the first to call it by that name), and then searched for a place to cross the Pecos. Like the Spanish explorers before them, the Hays expedition experienced much difficulty at the Pecos. They finally got across the river, probably a few miles below the modern Pandale Crossing, but after they could not find water west of the Pecos, they made a dash for the Rio Grande, and found it somewhere west of Langtry, probably in the vicinity of Lozier Canyon.

The Hays expedition finally got to Presidio del Norte, but it took them so long that they did not attempt to proceed farther. They headed back to San Antonio, crossed the Pecos, probably near Live Oak Creek, and passed well north of the rugged country near the mouth of the Pecos.

Texas having become a state in 1846, the U.S. government became interested in the southern boundary formed by the Rio Grande, and the secretary of war ordered that a feasible route for military traffic be established between San Antonio and Santa Fe. Lieutenant William Whiting was selected to lead an expedition to find a route, and his group, with Richard Howard, who had served as a scout with the Hays expedition, proceeded westward from San Antonio in February 1849. The group traveled well north of the dreaded canyonlands of the lower Pecos, establishing a route through passable terrain and adequate waterways, which later became known as the San Antonio–El Paso road. The trail they blazed went from San Felipe Springs, across Devils River, then across open country to the upper reaches of Devils River, over a divide to Howard Spring (named after Richard Howard), on to Live Oak Canyon, Comanche Springs, and on westward.[3]

Even though a satisfactory route had been found westward, much of the territory west of the Pecos was still unexplored. In June 1853, Lieutenant Nathaniel Michler headed an exploratory expedition into the lower trans-Pecos to complete the survey of the Rio Grande. Michler and his party followed the El Paso road to what he called Pecos Springs, which must have been near present Sheffield. From Pecos Springs, their destination was the Rio Grande, but the terrain to the south was so rough they could not proceed in that direction with their wagons; therefore, they made a circuitous westward trip to King's Springs and from there proceeded southeasterly to Independence Creek. Michler described Independence Creek as:

> a beautiful stream, running boldly among the hills, and is fed by innumerable springs bursting out from its banks. It is a rich treat for the eye in that arid country. Besides a copious supply of fresh, clear water, there is more timber than is ordinarily found upon streams draining these high plains; mezquite trees grow in large numbers for miles around, and the valley furnishes luxuriant grazing for animals. This place is much frequented by the Indians; an oasis in a desert country.[4]

Michler's group traveled from Independence Creek southward to what was later named Myers Springs, which he described as "a favorite camping place of the Indians; the many paintings of men and animals found covering the rocks, testify to their rude attempts in the artistic line." The explorers turned their wagons southward from Myers Springs and followed the Indian trail to a fordable crossing on the Rio Grande that he called Lipan Crossing. In a report, Michler stated:

> The Lipans often visited us here, and made themselves useful as guides. As it proved to be impracticable to conduct the survey on

land without taking an interminable length of time, it was decided to make the attempt in the bed of the river; anticipating such an emergency, boats had been built at San Antonio and brought along in wagons. After they had been put together and launched, and everything in readiness, the train was sent back by the road to Eagle Pass, there to meet the small party selected to descend the river to the same point. Upon trial, we found the boats, which were our only resource, would float—the only thing that could be said in their favor. The wood of which they were made was only partially seasoned, and the hot sun had so warped them, that they presented anything but a ship-shape appearance. The two skiffs were frail—a moderate blow would have knocked a hole in them—and the flat-boat was unwieldy and unmanageable. The current was so strong that the two good oarsmen could not stem it in a light skiff. At the point of embarkation was a short break in the canon of a few hundred feet on both sides of the river; the water then again rushed between rocky banks ten or twelve feet high, which increased in height as we proceeded. It would seem incredible that the bed of the stream could have been formed through ledges of solid rock. The occurrence of a freshet whilst encamped on its banks, however, convinced me of the impetuosity of its waters, which appeared to force everything before them. The bed is narrow, and hemmed in by continuous and perfect walls of natural masonry, varying from 50 to 300 feet in height; the breadth of the river being extremely contracted, these structures, seen from our boats, look stupendous as they rise perpendicularly from the water. It is not infrequently the case that we travel for miles without being able to find a spot on which to land. The limestone formation is capped by an infinite number of hills, about 150 feet in height, and of every imaginable shape. The whole adjacent country is traversed by deep arroyos or canons, intended by nature to drain the high plains bordering on the river; they are, in their appearance, but miniature creations of the same power which forced a passage for the Rio Grande. Their junctions with the river form large rapids or falls, caused by the rocks and earth matter washed down them. These rapids are numerous, many of them dangerous, and will always prove insurmountable obstructions to future navigation. The force of the current is very great, and for thirty miles above the mouth of the Pecos is one continued rapid; its average rate is nearly six miles an hour. The width of the river varies from 80 to 300 feet, and at a few points narrows down to 25 or 30; when confined between its rocky walls the channel is very deep. There are no tributaries along this section of the work, but several fine springs contrast their clear blue with the muddy waters of the river. There is but little growth until the approach to the mouth of the Pecos; a narrow strip of soil is then occasionally found at the base of the rocks, and gives forth to some fine live-oak and mesquite trees; grape-vines flourish in abundance, yielding a very palatable fruit; Catfish were the only kind of fish caught, some of them very large and heavy. Soft-shell turtle abound. But few varieties of game were seen; the wild turkey in large numbers, and some few deer—the latter of the black-tail species. The only practicable way of making the survey through the canyon was by allowing the boats to drop down the channel, taking the direction of the courses and timing the passage from bend to bend; when opportunity offered, the speed of each boat was ascertained by distances accurately measured on land, making allowances for change of current and other causes of error.

Observations for time and latitude were taken every night to check the work. On arriving at the mouth of the Pecos the survey, 125 miles in extent, was completed. The Pecos is more deserving of its other Mexican name, "Puerco," for it is truly a rolling mass of red mud, the water tasting like a mixture of every saline ingredient; its banks are like those of the Rio Grande for some distance above its mouth, and then become low and flat. As we continue to float down stream we find the country below the junction undergoes some very considerable changes; these become still more apparent on reaching the San Pedro or Devils River, whose waters form a dividing line between two distinct portions of country. The banks of the Rio Grande here present an entirely new appearance—they become low, and prairie land, covered with mesquite, extends as far as the eye can see; numerous well timbered and beautiful streams unite their waters with the river along this portion. Within a few hours of each other, both the party in charge of the train and the boat party reached Fort Duncan, near Eagle Pass, 110 miles by the river below the mouth of the Pecos.[5]

As exploration and settling by whites continued in western Texas and traffic toward the Pacific Ocean increased, the Indians became more alarmed and waged war with increased fury. Military protection had to be provided for the area along the San Antonio–El Paso road.

In 1852, after Texas had become a state, the U.S. government, concerned with the welfare of people living in western Texas, established Fort Clark, about one hundred miles east of the Pecos. It was expected that patrols from this fort could partially protect travelers on the San Antonio–El Paso trail. The trail had become a mail route in 1850 when Henry Skillman received a contract to carry mail from San Antonio to El Paso. Indians were a severe problem along the trail, and it required thirty days for the stagecoach to carry the mail over this tortuous six hundred-mile route.[6]

Some of the Jumanos and Comanches, like the Indians described by Lieutenant Michler, were friendly, but most of the Indians west of the Pecos fiercely attacked wagon trains and stagecoaches. The situation became so serious that in 1854 Fort Davis was established to discourage Indian interference; however, Fort Davis and Fort Clark were more than three hundred miles apart, and it was impossible for patrols from the two forts to protect the ever increasing flow of traffic between the two points. In 1855, Fort Lancaster was established about halfway between the two forts, to be followed by the establishment of Camp Hudson, in 1857, Fort Stockton, and Camp Del Rio. Soldiers were also occasionally stationed at Howard Well, forty-eight miles east of Fort Lancaster.

Colonel J. K. F. Mansfield, after inspecting Camp Lancaster, described the problems along the San Antonio–El Paso trail in a report. He wrote:

> Indians in this locality are marauding parties of Apaches and Mescaleros as highway men, and murderers. They keep out of sight and commit depredations and murders at times when least expected. They are on the Pecos, in the mountains, on Devils river, and are always concealed and difficult to find. The night after I left Capt. Lindsay at the 1st crossing on his return from Devils river, say 80 miles from Fort Clark, I encamped at the 2nd crossing, and a large cow and calf train bound for New Mexico, which encamped

5 miles ahead of me, was attacked and one man killed and another badly wounded and they were so disorganized when I came up to them in the morning having but four men left, as to make it necessary to detach 5 of my escort to accompany them to Camp Lancaster where through the assistance of Capt. Granger they were rested and refitted and furnished with an escort to Fort Davis. But for my timely arrival, and the aid of this post, these men would have been murdered and their cows and calves, so important to the inhabitants of New Mexico, captured by the Indians. The number of these Indians cannot be estimated. They do not occupy the ground permanently, but come from a distance, and it is quite probable that this and other posts will have to be maintained for a great many years.

This post is well located, being about ½ way between Forts Davis and Clark; and with some assistance from the quartermaster, can be made comfortable. It was established on the 21st August 1855, by Capt. Carpenter of the 1st Inft. who was relieved by Capt. Granger on the 1st Feb. 1856.

The officers are quartered in temporary adobe houses. There is a good parade and flag staff and two small gardens attempted by the companies, but the season here is so dry it will be difficult to raise vegetables.

Two companies are ample here, but they should have their officers and one of them should be mounted on mules, at will, so as to be able to trail Indians after they had committed depredations and follow them up and particularly at this place would the new rifled musket be available, for Indians when running must be reached at a long range, up the mountains etc., or not at all. An ambulance is indispensable here too. It is quite probable there is wood enough in this vicinity to last for several years; when further explorations towards the mouth of the Pecos might lead to timber. Capt. Granger is anxious to make an exploration of this kind and thinks he could turn the road down the Pecos, thereby avoiding long marches without water and saving some 30 or 40 miles by coming into the present road about 2nd or 1st crossing of Devils River.[7]

On August 18, 1856, the U.S. Congress passed the Postal Route Bill, providing for a mail route from San Antonio, Texas to San Diego, California. Postmaster general Aaron Brown on June 22, 1857 awarded a mail contract to James E. Birch to carry the mail twice each month over the 1,475-mile route between the two cities. The contract, for a period of four years, paid Birch $149,800 per year. The route, one writer said, went "from no place through nothing to nowhere." Under the schedule that was set up, thirty days was allowed for the trip. There was still no wagon road across the Pecos River near its mouth, and the mail route, as planned, would have to take the circuitous route up Devils River, by Fort Lancaster, and on to Fort Stockton.

On July 9, 1857 the first mail to be carried under the new contract left San Antonio accompanied by a group of men driving mules for use at relay stations to be established at the army posts between San Antonio and El Paso. The group progressed nicely until they reached the Devils River, where they were attacked by Indians. A detachment of cavalry came to their aid, but one man was killed and several mules were driven off by the Indians.

Birch died soon after the mail service was begun and George H. Giddings of San Antonio and R. E. Doyle took over the mail contract. The price for riding the bouncing, dusty stage from San Antonio to the West Coast was $200, meals included; the fare from San Antonio to El Paso was $100, but lodging was not included and these passengers had to rest as best they could. The stage, using Concord coaches drawn by a team of mules, left San Antonio on the ninth and twenty-fourth of each month at six in the morning and usually arrived in San Diego in fewer than thirty days.

Few passengers rode the stage between San Antonio and El Paso: most transcontinental travelers took the Butterfield Stage route that passed further north and the San Antonio–El Paso service lasted only about two years. It was then shortened and service was provided only from San Antonio to Fort Stockton. As the Civil War threatened, the route was discontinued completely.

A spring-fed watering hole on Howard Draw had been a camping spot frequented by Indians for centuries, but many times during long, hot summers it was dry. A well was dug so that water would always be available. Howard Draw, Howard Springs, and Howard Well were named after Richard Howard, the scout who had been so instrumental in finding the route across the Pecos. As travel increased on the San Antonio–El Paso road, soldiers from Fort Lancaster and Camp Hudson attempted to patrol the area near Howard Well, and several skirmishes were fought in that vicinity. The available force could not adequately patrol so many miles of rough country, and in April 1872 a wagon-train massacre occurred about a mile west of Howard Well. Accounts about the massacre are scant, and they vary, but it is generally believed that the wagon train consisted of six wagons. August Santleben, a freighter who carried goods from San Antonio to El Paso and Chihuahua City, wrote:

> My train nooned at Howard Well the following day and as it was about to move forward, Anastacio Gonzales drove into camp with his six wagons. He was a citizen of San Antonio and I knew him well, it was natural that I should stop to talk to him with the intention of getting him on his guard, against the dangers that lurked in that vicinity. I told him about the Indians who had watched my camp during my stay at the Salt Lake, and that they followed my train until the day before. I urged him to be careful and to use every precaution to avoid an attack, because I was satisfied the Indians were hovering in the neighborhood, and if they ceased to follow my wagons possibly they would make an assault on his camp if they saw that they could do so with impunity . . . .
>
> I did not hear of the disaster that overwhelmed Gonzales until I arrived at Ft. Clark. There I learned that Lieut. Vinson, with a detachment of troops, was scouting in that country and stopped at Howard's Well soon after Gonzales and all his men were killed. The wagons were still burning and the charred body of Gonzales was found secured to one of them, where evidently he was bound when still alive.
>
> Vinson immediately followed the trail of the Indians until he overtook them, and a fight occurred in which he and several of the soldiers were killed.[8]

Indians frequently harassed travelers making their way through the country between Fort Lancaster and Camp Hudson. Because of the roughness of the country, they were able to hide easily and escape easily. Consequently, more minor fights with the Indians occurred on that stretch of road than anywhere else along the San Antonio–El Paso road.

In an interview, Beula Farley told me that in 1874 her parents, Mr. and Mrs. J. D. Burdwell, were returning to Texas from Fort Lincoln, New Mexico, and as they approached Fort Lancaster, some black soldiers stopped them. The soldiers advised the Burdwells that a wagon train had been attacked on the west side of the Pecos, a little below Camp Lancaster, and the people had been massacred. As the Burdwells passed the massacre site, they saw the remains of the wagon train. For some reason the Burdwells had chosen not to go by the main road leading up the hill from Fort Lancaster and on to Howard Well; they were traveling on the little-used road that followed the Pecos to where Howard Draw emptied into the river.[9]

Soon after the rush to find gold in California in 1849, the need for a railroad linking the two coasts, east and west, was realized. Preliminary surveys by the U.S. War Department between 1850 and 1860 showed that it would be practical for a railroad to cross the trans-Pecos region of Texas. However, before a railroad could be constructed, the Indians would have to be driven out of the area.

Soldiers from Fort Davis, Fort Stockton, Fort Clark, and Camp Hudson, although in constant pursuit of the Indians, were unable to curtail their activities. Colonel William Shafter was charged with getting rid of the Indians, but delegated much of the responsibility to Lieutenant John Lapham Bullis.

Bullis, a native of New York, had fought in the Civil War. Captured at Gettysburg, he was later involved in a prisoner-of-war exchange. By the age of twenty-three, he had risen from private to captain, through a combination of merit and experience. Discharged from the army after the war, he enlisted again and was appointed a second lieutenant in the Forty-first U.S. Infantry on September 3, 1867. Two years later, Lieutenant Bullis was transferred to the Twenty-fourth Infantry, where he served under Colonel R. S. Mackenzie. In March 1873, he was placed in charge of the Seminole scouts stationed at Fort Clark and while commanding this unit, became noted as one of the greatest fighters of Indians in the Southwest.

The young lieutenant was in unusual circumstances. The Seminole scouts were descendants of runaway slaves and Seminole Indians. The Seminole Indians of Florida, disgusted with the Creek domination to which they were subjected, were happy to welcome the runaways in order to bolster their strength. In 1849 and 1850, several hundred Seminole Indians and blacks followed two chiefs, an Indian, Chief Wild Cat, and a black, Chief John Horse, into Mexico, but many of them were discontented there. Slavery, meantime, had been abolished in the United States, and at about the same time, the United States government was desperately in need of scouts on the Texas frontier; thus, it was agreed that the Seminoles would work for the cavalry as scouts if the government would pay expenses to the United States for able-bodied men and would furnish pay, provisions for their families, and grants of land. The scouts were headquartered at Fort Clark, where Lieutenant Bullis took command of the group. The scouts never numbered more than fifty men.[10]

Shortly after Bullis received the Seminole command, a band of Kickapoo, Lipan, and Mescalero Apaches made a devastating foray up the Nueces Valley. (It was believed that these same Indians had committed the massacre at Howard Well about a year earlier.) After making their Nueces Valley foray, they returned to their hideout near the village of Remolina, about sixty miles south of the Rio Grande. Colonel Mackenzie brazenly decided to destroy the settlement in Mexico in an effort to stop the Indians from raiding in the United States and then dashing to security below the border.

On the evening of May 17, 1873, after a couple of weeks of special training and preparation for the secret mission, Colonel Mackenzie and Second Lieutenant Bullis left Fort Clark with six companies of cavalry and a detachment of twenty Seminole scouts. They crossed the Rio Grande near the mouth of Las Moras Creek and rode all night toward the Indian village. The group reached the Indian hideout—which was actually three Indian villages—shortly after daylight, and made an old-fashioned, hell-for-leather cavalry charge that took the Indians by surprise. The Indians fled, but at least nineteen warriors were killed and others were captured, including Costillientos, the main Lipan chief. The U.S. forces lost only one man in the attack.

Mackenzie's forces burned one of the villages and shortly after noon headed back toward the Rio Grande. They rode all night, their second without sleep, and were back on U.S. soil the next morning. Mackenzie had gambled and won and there were no adverse repercussions from the U.S. authorities. Partly as a result of his gallantry in the skirmish south of the border, Bullis was promoted to first lieutenant on June 20, 1873.[11]

The Indians living in Mexico who raided settlements and wagon trains north of the Rio Grande were soon to develop a great fear of Lieutenant John Bullis. He and his scouts chased many marauding groups of Indians back to their villages in Mexico. In a report on one of these raids, dated May 1875, he wrote:

We left the springs at about 1 o'clock PM and marched east for about three miles and struck a fresh trail going Northwest toward Eagle's Nest Crossing. The trail was quite large and came from the direction of the settlements, and was made, I judge by 75 head or more of horses. We immediately took the trail and followed it briskly for about an hour and came upon a party of Indians unob-served, attempting to cross the Pecos to the West side. We immedi-ately tied our horses, and crept back of a bush, up to within seventy-five yards of them (all of which were dismounted except one squaw) and gave them a volley which we followed up lively for about three-quarters of an hour during which time we twice took their horses from them and killed three Indians and wounded a fourth. We were at last compelled to give way, as they were about to get around us and cut us off from our horses. I regret to say that I lost mine with saddle and bridle complete, and just saved my hair by jumping on my sergeant's horse, back of him. The truth is, there were some 25 or 30 Indians in all, and mostly armed with Winchester guns, and they were too much for us.[12]

The scouts with Lieutenant Bullis at the battle near the mouth of the Pecos were Sergeant John Ward, Trumpeter Isaac Payne, and Trooper Pompey Factor. The three men received the Congressional Medal of Honor for their participation in the battle and the rescue of the lieutenant. As Bullis leaped onto Ward's horse, the Indians opened heavy fire on the group, particularly on the sergeant and the lieutenant. A bullet cut Ward's carbine sling and a ball shattered the stock of his saddle.

Since most of Bullis's action was west of the Pecos, he established a headquarters at Myers Springs, a few miles northeast of the present town of Dryden. Bullis and his men built a rock tank around the springs and erected two stone buildings and several adobe structures on the drill-field above the springs. The two main traveled trails of the lower trans-Pecos met at Myers Springs: one road came from the mouth of Howard Draw, up Fielder Canyon to Myers Springs, and the other came from the mouth of the Pecos. The two trails joined to form the road westward. It was a strategic spot for the location of Bullis's headquarters west of the Pecos, for it was a large spring located in a barren area, and Indian trails from north, east, south, and west converged at the cool, clear spring. Extensive Indian pictographs and mounds of burned rock indicated that Indians had used the spring for hundreds of years.

The exact dates that Bullis and his scouts occupied Myers Springs is not known, but we do know—through a tale told by my father, Guy Skiles—that the group spent at least one lonely Christmas at the outpost. My father had come west from San Antonio in 1904 with his father, Jim Skiles, a cowboy and carpenter. Dad began working on ranches on both sides of the Rio Grande at an early age and was among the last of the old-time cowboys of the area who lived on the open range. Guyo, as he was called, married Vashti Barnes, a Langtry schoolteacher in 1929 and lived in the Langtry area until his death in 1986. He had a strong interest in the history of the area and frequently asked old-timers about their experiences. He told me about having worked with Pompey Factor, who had been with Bullis at Myers Springs:

> Pompey was an old, old fellow when I knew him in 1911. He cooked for us on a cow outfit near Brackettville. I remember him telling about being with Bullis one Christmas at Myers Springs.
>
> He and the other scouts wanted to go back to their homes at Brackettville for Christmas. I don't know how many scouts there were, but Bullis felt that he could only let one of the Seminoles go home for Christmas, so he told Pompey and the other scouts to go out and hunt deer and the one that brought back the biggest deer would go home for Christmas.
>
> Pompey brought in the biggest deer, so early the next morning he saddled up his horse and took off down the trail for Brackettville, which was about a hundred and fifty miles away. When he got down on the Pecos River near the mouth of Fielder Draw, he ran into a bunch of Indians, and they chased him almost all the way back to Myers Springs. Pompey said he decided he would just stay at Myers Springs for Christmas.[13]

Bullis and his Seminole scouts stayed on the trail of the Indians from March 1873 until June 1881. During this period, Bullis led his men on at least twenty-five major operations against hostile Indians. One such incident occurred in July 1876 when Bullis and Shafter crossed the Rio Grande near the present site of Langtry and rode south into Mexico for five or six days.

While the main body of soldiers rested, Bullis and his scouts and about twenty troopers went ahead to locate the Indian encampment. At dawn on July 30, Bullis attacked the Lipan village and after fierce hand-to-hand fighting, captured and burned the village. Fourteen braves were killed, four squaws were captured, and about one hundred horses and mules were taken. This time the retreat nearly proved disastrous, for Bullis's small detachment was pursued by a much superior force of the regular Mexican army, who resented the American intrusion into their country. Shafter, with three hundred troopers, rejoined Bullis in the nick of time, and the angry Mexicans, after sullen negotiations, allowed the U.S. force to continue across the Rio Grande.[14]

In October 1877, Bullis again crossed the Rio Grande in pursuit of marauding Indians and cornered some Apaches with stolen horses in a canyon. When the Indians proved too strong for Bullis and his small force, he recrossed the river, but returned seven days later with reinforcements. The larger group attacked the Indians and after recovering some of the stolen loot, burned the village. They returned safely across the Rio Grande.[15]

As Bullis continued his operations west of the Pecos River, it became more and more evident that a wagon crossing near the mouth of the Pecos was needed. Bullis decided that the most feasible place to cross the Pecos gorge would be at the Indian crossing near the mouth of the Pecos, where he and his scouts had fought Indians in 1875. Bullis and his scouts took time out from hunting Indians to begin building the wagon road across the Pecos in 1878. He built a road crossing the Pecos a short distance above the confluence of the Pecos and Rio Grande, but the road was rough, narrow, and steep. In the early winter of 1879, Captain Charles McNaugh, of the Twentieth Infantry, supervised additional road work at the Pecos, which he described in a letter of October 26 of that year:

> This command commenced work where it was left by Capt. Fletcher's command and completed the extension to the river on the 23rd, since which time we have been working on the other side. It will take from 30 to 35 days to work to the top of the bluff. The road built last summer has settled considerably and should be repaired, especially upon the grade down the side of the bluff where in some places the available road bed is 7 ft. 10 inches wide. These places can be widened by blasting further into the bluff. I think

12 days labor can be used to very good advantage in making these repairs.[16]

Bullis was well respected by his Seminole scouts. Years later, Joseph Phillips, one of the scouts, was quoted as saying of his commanding officer:

> The scouts thought a lot of Bullis. Lieutenant Bullis was the only officer ever did stay the longest with us. That fella suffer jest like we all did out in de woods. He was a good man. He was a Injun fighter. He was tuff. He didn't care how big a bunch dey wuz, he went into 'em every time, but he looked after his men. His men was on equality too. He didn't stan' back and say "Go yonder," he would say, "Come on, boys, let's go get 'em." [17]

During the eight years that Bullis fought Indians west of the Pecos, he also earned the deep respect of the tough West Texans that he was protecting. Prominent landmarks such as Bullis Gap, west of Sanderson, and Bullis Crossing on the Pecos were named after the hard-fighting lieutenant. Bullis's ability was recognized by his commanding officers, too: in 1904 he was a brigadier general. In recommending Bullis for promotion, Brigadier General D. S. Stanley declared that Bullis's career in southwest Texas was the most successful of any Indian fighter in the history of the U.S. Army.

Artist Frederick Remington paid a tribute to Bullis after he had been placed in charge of the San Carlos Indian Reservation in Arizona. In an 1889 magazine article, Remington drew this word picture:

> The affairs of the San Carlos agency are administered at present by an army officer, Captain Bullis, of the Twenty-fourth Infantry. As I have observed him in the discharge of his duties, I have no doubt that he pays high life insurance premiums. He does not seem to fear the beetle-browed pack of murderers with whom he has to deal, for he has spent his life in command of Indian scouts and not only understands their character, but has gotten out of the habit of fearing anything. If the deeds of this officer had been on civilized battle fields instead of in silently leading a pack of savages over the desert wastes of the Rio Grande, they would have gotten him his niche in the Temple of Fame. But they are locked up in the gossip of

the army mess-room, and end in the soldiers' matter-of-fact joke about how Bullis used to eat his provisions in the field, by opening a can a day from the pack, and whether it was peaches or corned-beef, making it suffice. The Indians regard him as almost supernatural, and speak of the "Whirlwind" with many grunts of admiration, as they narrate his wonderful achievements.[18]

In 1881, after the Indians had been driven from the trans-Pecos country, Bullis was presented with a gold sword by the citizens of West Texas as a token of their appreciation for his service to them. Colonel Martin L. Crimmins, in an article in the *Army and Navy Courier*, November 1926, described the famous sword:

It is certainly the finest sword ever presented in this part of the country to a military hero. The sword was made by the famous firm of Bent & Bus, of Boston. The hilt and scabbard is fire-gilded and most elaborately and appropriately ornamented and inscribed. The hilt is the Goddess of Liberty and the American Eagle combined. The guard is illustrated with a camp scene in the Chinati Mountains; then follows the inscription, "He protected our homes—our homes were open to him." Then lengthwise on the scabbard, "Presented to John L. Bullis by the people of Western Texas."

By the time of Bullis's departure—about a year before the arrival of Roy Bean—he and his fellow members of the military had finished removing the Indian threat from the trans-Pecos country. It was safe for the coming of the railroad and the settlers.

CHAPTER 3

———◆•◆———

BUILDING THE
RAILROAD

Men had dreamed of building a transcontinental railroad from Texas to California since about 1850, but Indians, the Civil War, and other problems had dashed even the best plans. By 1880, Texas was ready for the railroad that would connect the Gulf of Mexico with the Pacific Ocean: through the efforts of soldiers like Bullis and the Seminole scouts, most of the Indians had been driven out of the state; the state legislature had granted sixteen sections of land for each mile of railroad built; and the economy of the nation could support a railroad across the southern United States. Freight outfits like Roy Bean's were slow—and also like Bean's, undependable. Railroads were the coming thing.

The Galveston, Harrisburg, and San Antonio Railroad (G. H. & S. A.) reached San Antonio from the east in 1877 and was authorized by the State of Texas to extend its line to El Paso; the Southern Pacific was progressing eastward from San Francisco toward El Paso. C. P. Huntington, who controlled the Southern Pacific, also had a large interest in Col. Tom Pierce's G. H. & S. A. The two men decided that by joining forces they could have a transcontinental railroad. Immediately, they pushed construction in order to beat Jay Gould's Texas and Pacific railroad, which had the same objective.

Once plans had been finalized for the railroad, a suitable route through western Texas had to be found. Preliminary surveys conducted by the U.S. War Department had indicated the most feasible route for a railroad from San Antonio to El Paso would be via San Felipe Springs (present Del Rio), to Myers Springs (near the present village of Dryden) and around the southern edge of the Davis Mountains. M. J. Ripps assisted in the survey and we pick up his story as told to J. Marvin Hunter for his *The Trail Drivers of Texas:*

> In 1880 and 1881 I went on a trail of a different nature by becoming a member of a surveying outfit to blaze the right of way for the

Southern Pacific Railway from San Antonio west to the Rio Grande River. Two men joined the outfit with me at San Antonio, and the crew consisted of seventeen men. We surveyed as far as Uvalde, when we got orders to arm ourselves and keep our eyes "peeled" for Indians. This was too much for the two men who had joined with me, and so they quit. We continued the survey, and were about 128 miles west of San Antonio, when the government sent twenty soldiers to us as an escort. At the Nenecatchie Mountains we had our first experience with the redskins. They came in the night and tried to steal our mules and horses by stampeding them. We had our guards, or outposts, stationed some distance from camp and they exchanged shots, but none of our men were hurt. At San Felipe, on the Rio Grande, Rangers took the place of the soldiers and acted as our protectors. While we were camped at the McKenzie Crossing on the Rio Grande, the Indians made another attempt to get our horses, but were routed by the Rangers. From there on we did not see any more Indians until we came to Eagle's Nest, on the Rio Grande [the present site of Langtry]. We were camped some 350 feet above the level of the river bed, and were cutting out a trail wide enough for a burro to pass with a cask, or small barrel on either side, to transport water from the river. We had stopped for the noon hour when we noticed nine Indians, seven bucks and two squaws. They had evidently descended to the river bottom some miles above and were winding their way to a point directly in front of us, where they could get to the water. They were coming in single file, some ten feet apart, and were in full war paint, the Indians in the rear being the guard. The eight went to water to satisfy their thirst, while one stood guard. Then the guard went to drink while one of the squaws stood guard, and she spied us, as we could tell from her gestures. When she gave the alarm they took to their horses and disappeared up the river. As we were not looking for trouble, we did not fire at them, but doubled our guards to protect against an attack from the rear.

Our next camp was at Paint Cave. One night we sent our mules and horses out to grass with two guards in charge. Indians crept up and tried to scare the animals. One of the guards, finding that something was not right, gave the alarm, and the fireworks started. We fired some thirty or forty shots, and one of the guards claimed he got an Indian. This painted cave is worth a trip to see. It is a big opening under a protruding boulder, large enough for fourteen men to ride into on horseback at one time. Its inner walls are decorated with Indian paintings of wild animals, lions, tigers, buffaloes, etc., and all the sign language on the walls—some of which we could not understand if they were played on a phonograph.[1]

In May 1881, construction superintendent J. H. Strobridge, who was building the Southern Pacific, started laying rails eastward from El Paso under the auspices of the Galveston, Harrisburg, and San Antonio Railroad; meanwhile, since February, W. H. Monroe's men had been building a railroad westward from San Antonio. The two construction men hoped to join their rails a little more than a year later, but between them was a vast expanse of rugged land to cross. Strobridge had the expert help of Chinese laborers who had been with the Central Pacific in its conquest of the Sierra Nevada; Monroe had Irish, German, Italian, Mexican, and American men with a wide range of abilities.

The *Sacramento Daily Record-Union*, a California newspaper, carried on March 22, 1882, a front-page lead article datelined March 21, San Francisco:

> The Southern Pacific Railroad is being built through Texas as rapidly as possible. Two construction gangs, consisting in all of 2,000 men, are at work; one having started from El Paso, and the other working westward from San Antonio. It is thought that these two divisions will meet at the Pecos river, which is about 130 miles from San Antonio and 400 miles from El Paso. On the El Paso end of the line over 253 miles of track have been completed, and the work is going on at the rate of about a mile and a half a day. The country is wild and mountainous; deep ravines and gullies abound, and mountain streams run through precipitous canyons. A still worse country for railroad work will be met in about thirty days, if the present rate of construction is maintained, but the engineers will continue to push steadily forward as fast as possible. English steel rails are used in the construction of this road, and most of the supplies are brought from this city. A few things are obtained from Los

Angeles and the southern country, and some hay and forage for the stock are obtained by the men from the country through which they are passing.

By April 1, the G. H. & S. A. construction crews had reached Del Rio and it was estimated that three thousand men were working west of the new railroad town. The railroad proceeded westward from Del Rio and picked up momentum after it crossed Devils River. Construction then moved rapidly to Seminole Canyon. This canyon had a large, permanent water hole, so a camp was established there that would serve as the jumping off place for construction to the Pecos River, a few miles to the west. The camp had hardly been established, however, when the railroad builders began to learn about the importance of water in the barren region. The *San Antonio Weekly Express*, March 30, 1882 told of the water problems at Seminole Canyon: "The large water hole known as the Painted Cave and supposed to yield abundant supply for all demands, is fast diminishing, and unless it rains soon railroad contractors and the traveling public will have to haul and use water elsewhere. About ten railroad camps have been in the habit of getting their water here; train and other stock did the same, and much inconvenience would be felt if it should give out. Seminole Creek has abundant water below Painted Cave water hole, but almost inaccessible to wagons."

A short distance southwest of Seminole Canyon, the railroad met the Rio Grande. The tortuous descent along the Rio Grande to the mouth of the Pecos was begun. The Pecos River gorge was more than three hundred feet deep and almost two thousand feet wide. Railroad engineers considered it virtually impossible to span the chasm, so they decided that the only way the river could be crossed would be to build the railroad along the Rio Grande, gradually losing elevation, and reaching the Pecos at its confluence with the Rio Grande. The railroad would cross the Pecos on an ordinary bridge, barely above the high-water mark, and then continue westward along the Rio Grande, gaining elevation. The roadbed would finally leave the canyon of the Rio Grande about five miles west of the Pecos. The solution was not simple, because a number of deep canyons emptying into the Rio Grande on each side of the Pecos had to be crossed. On each side of the Pecos was a long section of sheer cliff that would be so difficult to traverse that engineers decided it would be more practical to blast tunnels parallel to the Rio Grande cliffs.

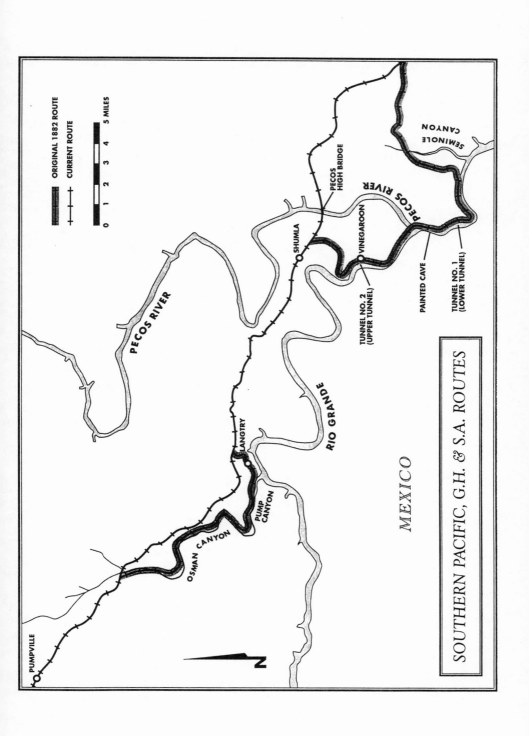

SOUTHERN PACIFIC, G.H. & S.A. ROUTES

Construction of a nearly level railroad through the rocky land cut by deep canyons was extremely difficult. Almost all of the work was done by hand or with teams of mules and scrapers. Some steam equipment was used, but it had to be anchored on concrete bases and was not portable. In order to cut through hills of rock, holes had to be dug with drill-bars and sledgehammers. It was a tortuous process, making a hole deep enough and large enough to hold a sizable charge of black powder. Two men worked together drilling the holes, one man holding the drill bar while the other pounded it with a sledge. The drillers developed a rhythm: one man would turn the drill-bar about one-half a turn, to keep it from sticking in the bottom of the hole, while the other man raised the hammer for another blow. If the rhythm was broken, time and energy were wasted. The holes were frequently cleaned out with an iron rod, shaped on the end to form a ladle for scooping out the pulverized rock. Once the holes were drilled to a sufficient depth, they were loaded with black powder by men called powder monkeys. Several holes were blasted at once and then the loose rocks were removed so that more holes could be drilled. Where it was feasible, teams pulling fresnos (large scrapers) were used to move the rocks, but much of the rubble had to be removed by hand. Rocks were lifted into two-wheeled carts pulled by mules and then dumped where fills were needed to cross canyons. Sometimes, men used baskets to carry the debris.[2]

A number of bridges had to be built over dry arroyos running into the Rio Grande—mostly wooden trestles resting on rock piers. A large force of stonecutters quarried limestone rock and prepared finely shaped blocks of stone from three to five feet square for use in the piers. To get these huge blocks of stone, the quarrymen drilled a series of holes in a straight line and then drove tapered iron wedges into the holes. After enough pressure had been exerted by the wedges, the huge block would break loose. It was then shaped with hammers and chisels. The masons took great pride in their work and often cut their initials into the blocks when they were completed. The stones were so perfectly fitted that very little mortar was necessary to hold them together; in fact, some of the footing at the ends of the bridges contained no mortar at all.

Building the roadbed along the Rio Grande from Seminole Canyon to Shumla, a distance of about twelve miles, was such a tremendous project that several contractors were brought in to build segments of the line. Construction camps, established on both sides of the Pecos, bore such

First railroad bridge across the Pecos, constructed in 1882. Lacking the technical ability to span the Pecos River gorge at the cliff top, engineers routed the railroad along the Rio Grande and crossed the Pecos at is mouth. This circuitous route was abandoned in 1892. (Photo courtesy of J. P. Calk.)

names as Tunnelville, Rocksolid, Hood's City, Monroesburg, Gageborough, Bernardale, and Vinegaroon. Tunnelville, a large camp about three miles east of the Pecos, was where tunnel number one was being blasted parallel to the Rio Grande. Vinegaroon was about four miles west of the Pecos, where tunnel number two was being dug.

As more than two thousand men began converging in the area near the mouth of the Pecos to work on the construction of the railroad, other people also moved in to relieve the laborers of their hard-earned dollars; dozens of tent saloons were established; gambling houses opened; dance-hall girls moved in; and Murillo's Circus opened at Monroe's lower camp (a venture that was not in competition with Bean: his saloon was at the upper tunnel). A saloon, or mescal shop, that served whiskey made from maguey plants opened on the Mexican side of the river, opposite Monroe's camp. Even the eighth cavalry had established a subpost at the mouth of the Pecos, and built a pontoon bridge across the river that could be used by the contractors. As thousands of hardened men massed in the area around the mouth of the Pecos, all sorts of crime was common and there was very little regard for human life.

The transcontinental railroad that would connect Texas and California was eagerly awaited by a large segment of the Texas population. San Antonio was two hundred miles from the Pecos River, but the *San Antonio Daily Express* regularly published articles about the construction progress. A series of accounts from that newspaper gives us glimpses of the problems encountered by construction workers in the summer of 1882:

Seminole Cave, June 12. It never rains west of San Antonio except when it wants to, then, as last night, it comes suddenly. Rain, hail, and wind paid us a sudden visit about sunset yesterday. Tents fell before the storm as easy prey. Seminole caves were filled with water where a bold current six or seven feet deep, swiftly flowed along toward the Rio Grande. At Yulick's Camp a water tank and wagon were washed away and carried some distance . . . .

HURRICANE ON THE PECOS

About 8:00 last Sunday night a terrific storm came upon the railroaders in camp at the Pecos, sweeping everything before it. It lasted nearly an hour during which torrents of water fell. The thunder and lightening were wonderfully severe. One of Hall's tents was struck and one man was killed and three sent swirling out of the tent in a senseless state. Henry and Dilley had their entire headquarters and camp, and over 100 tents at their works blown down. Max Meyer, who recently established a general supply store at this locality, had the roof blown off and all his goods wet. Damage is estimated to be at least $2,000.00. Ogleby and Company at the Pecos had their building to blow down and also sustained a loss of fully a thousand dollars. The government pontoon bridge across the Pecos River was torn loose at one end and swung around, sinking one boat. The Government is now repairing it, but all transportation except by ambulance has been delayed. Henry Ware Saloon on the Pecos was blown down and considerable damage done. Many other saloons and restaurants along the line of the road were blown down . . . .

Monroe's Third Camp, Mex. . . June 13. A gentleman whose name I learned from papers found in his valise shown me by Mr. J. Hall, to be Herman Wahlers at Texas House, Congress Street, Houston Texas got drowned while bathing in the Rio Grande. His companion who saw him drowning, took care of Wahler's moneys supposed to have amounted to about $170.00. This happened Sunday, June 11.

On the night of the same day during the storm, an Italian was struck by lightening and immediately killed. An order was at once made out signed W. H. Monroe per Smith and sent to the nearest store (Mr. Meyers) for lumber to give the unfortunate Italian a decent funeral. The drowned man's body has not been found.

With the remark "Men are more plentiful than lumber" the order was declined and not filled. The poor Italian still had no coffin, though he little knew the table he ate his supper on would be his coffin in the morning. The loss of the table to Mr. Monroe is a small matter. A larger matter will be the withdrawal of his custom from a house that does not fill his orders, for Mr. Monroe's every movement shows that what he needs for his men, they must have, shall get, whether they are in robust health or slain by a streak of lightening.

Mr. Smith, head clerk at this camp and J. Hall, in charge of the whole work, will cease issuing orders on the store nearest them.

Deputy Sheriff Young of Pecos County, has himself established near here and a few of the long promised rangers have come at last.

The late storms have done much damage at and from the Pecos westward. Whole camps were exposed to the fury of the storm with all tents blown over.

By the evening of June 15, the pontoon bridge had been put back in place, the Italian who had been struck by lightening was buried, and about seven thousand men were in what was then Pecos County, building the railroad.

The largest concentration of men on the west side of the Pecos was at the site where tunnel number two was being blasted parallel to the Rio Grande. Four long and high bridges were being built nearby to cross canyons entering the Rio Grande, and some deep cuts and high fills also were necessary to achieve a fairly level roadbed. The tent city of Vinegaroon, named after a scorpion-like insect commonly found under rocks in the area, sprang up on the rocky hill just above the tunnel. Many reports indicate that the construction camp of Vinegaroon was indeed a poisonous place. The hardworking, hard-living construction men were so tough that in June 1882 the contractors requested that Texas Rangers be sent to Vinegaroon to maintain order. A colorful description of Vinegaroon was printed in the December 28, 1882, issue of the *San Antonio Weekly Express:*

> Vinegaroon: This place is not down on the maps, and probably never will be. A month hence and it will be a city of the past. Six months ago the spot where it now stands was just a rocky hill, covered with a dark growth of sotallos, prickly pears, cat's claws, Spanish daggers and Lechegier. Then the nimble jack rabbit, the aesthetic centipede, the industrious tarantula and the pestiferous little beast in whose honor Vinegaroon is named were the sole inhabitants. Now it is a thriving community of perhaps two thousand persons, boasts of two stores, two barber shops, a bakery, five restaurants, a hotel, twenty-three saloons, and a dance hall, besides a justice of the peace [Judge Bean] and a company of rangers. Six months hence the aboriginal inhabitants will creep back, the thorny vegetation which characterized this Rio Grande Country will

Upper tunnel on the Rio Grande, about four miles west of the mouth of the Pecos. The tent city of Vinegaroon was located directly above this tunnel. (Photo courtesy of Willie Shaw.)

Raymond Skiles, the author's son, examines remains of a saloon building at Vinegaroon, located above the railroad tunnel on the west side of the Pecos. In 1882, the population of the village was about two thousand, but it was abandoned when the railroad was completed. The old roadbed, snaking along the Rio Grande, is in the background.

spring up again in rank luxuriance, even hiding the small mounds in the graveyard, which institution, by the way, is an indispensable and well patronized adjunct to a thriving frontier town. Fifteen years ago, towns like Vinegaroon were unknown in Texas, and were, from the very nature of things, an impossibility. They came with the railroad boom, which began in 1875 and the state is now full of them. They are the growth of a day; they flourish during their brief existence like a green bay tree, and disappear with the same comet-like abruptness which marked their advent.

Vinegaroon was spread out over two or three rocky hills covered with sotol and lechuguilla. There were only a few square feet of level space in the entire tent city. The men building the tunnel and the nearby bridges and deep cuts pitched their tents or threw down their bedrolls as close to their work as possible—bone tired after long hours of fighting the rock and heat. The saloons sprang up as entrepreneurs arrived, each with a wagonload of booze. There were so many saloons and competition was so fierce that reporters bragged that mixed drinks were cheaper in Vinegaroon than any place in the

United States. Ice was brought by train from San Antonio to the end of the railroad and then hauled by wagon to the camps. At that time, San Antonio was one of the major ice-manufacturing centers in the United States.

Vinagaroon early established the area's future association with the sport of boxing, foreshadowing Bean's later title fight venture: one of the centers of attraction at the camp was a boxing ring, in which local pugilists pounded at each other while the spectators bet drinks on the outcome. The tent village bloomed each payday, but even between paydays there was enough money in camp to keep things lively each evening.[3]

Officials of the G. H. & S. A. and the Southern Pacific were anxious to get the final link of railroad between Eagle Nest and Seminole Canyon completed. On April 17, 1882, Southern Pacific officials Charles Crocker, J. E. Gray, William Hood, and J. H. Strobridge met Jim Converse, the chief engineer of the G. H. & S. A. at the Seminole camp. The following day, they inspected the construction sites between Seminole Canyon and Shumla. At that time there was still a gap of about one hundred miles between the two projects, and the inspection team wanted a first-hand look so they might hasten completion of the railroad.[4] The completion of the two tunnels, numerous cuts through solid rock, and several bridges was a slow process, and a month after the inspection, an impatient Pierce, president of the G. H. & S. A., made his own inspection of the construction sites. The *San Antonio Daily Express* issue of June 1, 1882 reported:

> May 26, Colonel Pierce and Major Converse passed through Seminole Cave Monday last, on their way west. Their object was to inspect the progress of the works and promote their rapid completion.
>
> Although everything is working at high pressure under the direction of able and trustworthy men, the presence of the president could not fail to have a good effect and give impetus to the work. The worthy president did not appear to be enamored of a buggy ride over jolty wagon roads up and down the rocky canyons of the Rio Grande. Nor did he appreciate the comforts and luxury of a railroad camp of the far west, but he put a cheerful countenance on the matters well knowing that he would return to the comforts of civilized life with that increased zest and appreciation which short privation can only give. It would be safe to predict that

when he again views the grand scenery of the Rio Grande it will be from a window of his luxurious palace car but his colleague, Maj. Converse is so accustomed to the discomforts incidental to railroading that he hardly feels or even notices them. A meal hastily swallowed after a long journey, an hours beautiful sleep, with or without fleas, then to work on the road.

"Keep moving" is his motto. "The road must be through in twenty days; more men; more powder; quick! Rend me a path through these limestone cliffs in less time, or well, I'll put somebody else there."

The air at the mouth of the Pecos and up and down the Rio Grande resounds with the sounds of the drill; explosions and gunpowder and dynamite continually echoes from bluff to bluff, day and night (here the bluffs are from two hundred to three hundred feet in height). The wagon road is busy with teams hauling supplies and gunpowder, while troops of sturdy men of all nations press to the front to fight against rude nature. There are dark spots in the pleasure—the whiskey dens. The habitat of loathsome fungiis in the neighborhood of large contractors, camps or frequented crossroads, near or where ever workmen pass to and fro.

A bit of canvass, a few sticks, with the flower stalks of the sotol supply, ready at hand, a dismal coal oil lamp, some batter cups, and a barrel or two from the whiskey dens and the stock in trade. One may scent it from afar, for when in full blast, the atmosphere is furious with blasphemy and ringing of pistol shots. The poisoned victim soon becomes moneyless and is cast into the road a sodden, filthy, degraded brute; or as the demon, 40-rod whiskey, enters into him he may be a dangerous, maddened beast, ready to kill friend or foe, and often does. Verily the crime and misery caused by these numerous whiskey dens are past belief. Surely this would be a fitting sphere for the missionary temperance, or otherwise, but as there is neither money nor notoriety to get from the work here, only privations and some danger, the evils are not likely to be met by the modern type of apostle.

Here the report raises the issue that would lead to Roy Bean's becoming the Law West of the Pecos—the need, felt by some of the people living in the area, for a resident representative of the law. The dispatch continued:

> We want some official armed with summary jurisdiction outside to allow the path of ordinary civil law. A military officer with such authority and able to make it respected with the force at his command, would convert the Pecos crossing from the pandemonium to a comparatively orderly place and would indirectly expedite the progress of the railway works.

A construction army consisting of an estimated seven thousand men worked six days a week from seven in the morning until six in the evening through the hot summer of 1882. On their day off, the workers spent their time drinking, gambling, resting, or fishing. The easiest way to get fish from the Pecos or the Rio Grande was to kill them with explosives, which were plentiful. On one occasion that summer, one "fisherman" shattered both his arms when a blast occurred before he got the explosive in the water.[5]

The hard limestone slowly yielded to the hordes of workmen and on August 24, 1882 a momentous report was published in the *San Antonio Weekly Express* telling about the tunnel three miles east of the mouth of the Pecos:

FIRST RAILROAD TUNNEL IN TEXAS IS COMPLETED

> River Bend Camp: Mr. Joseph L. Parr . . . civil engineer of the G. H. & S. A. R. R. . . . has just completed the first tunnel ever built in Texas. In a letter to a friend . . . Mr. Parr says: "I wish you all could have been here to see the ceremonies, etc., when we got daylight through. There were Italians on one side and Germans on the other. In pursuance of etiquette I was the first to pass through— followed by my first assistant, the principal contractor, the subcontractor, the foreman and lastly the men, the shovel and pick that did the last work being borne by myself and first assistant in procession up to my camp, and there placed in front of my tent decorated with Italian, German, Mexican, and American colors and illuminated with lanterns. Here in the bright moonlight we clustered

The first railroad tunnel built in Texas. Photo shows the western end of the lower tunnel. The line runs parallel to the Rio Grande, about three miles downstream from the mouth of the Pecos. A man swings on the rope ladder leading up the cliff to the River Bend Camp, a boistrous tent-village where construction workers lived. (Photo courtesy of J. P. Calk.)

around my tent on the gray and barren rocks of the Rio Grande under the balmy moonlight, and sang Italian, German, and English
songs for two or three hours, and all went to our slumbers peace-
fully and happy. The next evening I was serenaded chorally by the
Italians and the Germans.

Laborers on the road are now plentiful, almost too many, if a
reduction of a price from $2.75 to $2.00 per day is any indication
of that.

While G. H. & S. A. workmen along the Pecos were tediously carving a
roadbed out of solid rock and spanning the deep canyons, the crews at the
Southern Pacific end of the line steadily progressed eastward. Strobridge, the
S. P. superintendent of construction, who had earlier built the first transcontinental railroad and, as mentioned earlier, still had some of the Chinese
pick-and-shovel men who had helped him in the Sierra Nevada, had also
brought additional laborors from China. In all, he had more than three
thousand Chinese building the railroad in West Texas. He also employed
more than five hundred anglos. This huge force reached Sanderson in May
1882 and rapidly moved on eastward.

The Chinese laborers established sizable camps near the construction,
and life in the Chinese camps was in accordance with their lifestyles in China.
Hot tea was always available and cooking was done in large, cast-iron woks.
Some of the men camped in tents and others simply slept under the stars.
Personal belongings were generally kept in carpetbags and small chests.
Opium smoking was very much a part of life to these men working far from
their homeland. The opium was brought from China in brass containers,
about one and one-half inches high and three inches square and was used
in opium lamps—also made in China. Tiger whiskeys from China were
occasionally found in the camps, but the men also consumed American
alcoholic beverages. Much of the trading and gambling in the Chinese camps
was done with brass Chinese coins, each with its square hole in the center.

A dispatch in the *San Antonio Daily Express* of October 11, 1882 described
the Chinese camps:

> Special from Eaglenest. Your correspondent has just visited
> Strowbridges [sic] Chinese camp. There are located upwards of
> 2,500 Chinese and about 400 white laborers. A remarkable outfit

of good machinery, etc., about 700 good horses and 400 wagons & carts. Mr. Strowbridge has built the road from the California end and has built it rapidly and almost without expense. Powder alone costing almost as much as a contractor would ordinarily have spent for the entire work, but speed and not expense has been the main point. Many workmen are now engaged in hauling bridge material from the end of the track to the site of the bridge at Eagle Nest, and the bridge will go up rapidly.

Strowbridge sends back all Chinese except plate layers when he completes track to the nest.

The Chinese are treated more like slaves than anything else, they are drove round and sometimes used severely, if they don't work to suit the bosses. The "Eagle Nest City" has grown small owing to the many camps being removed. The possibilities for the future point to it as a site of a railroad depot and a town of some importance.

The reporter, Fred Locker, went on to mention two other camps near Strobridge's—those of W. H. Monroe and J. C. Hood. The Strobridge camp was located about two miles west of Eagle Nest on a long flat overlooking the roadbed. It was a movable city, complete with blacksmith shop and laundry.

Eagle Nest—the name being the first given to the place overlooking the Rio Grande that would later be called Langtry—was an important point on the railroad because of the abundance of water at Torres Spring, located in a deep canyon running into the Rio Grande just west of Eagle Nest.

Water was very important to the railroad builders because the steam locomotives would need huge amounts of water when the railroad was completed. Eagle Nest City became a large construction camp, and many of the road builders were diverted at that point to building a rock dam at Torres Springs. A steam-driven pump was to be installed there, to provide water for the locomotives.

By October 1, 1882, many contractors working in the vicinity of Eagle Nest were finishing their jobs. The *San Antonio Weekly Express* of September 21, 1882, reported from Eagle Nest:

Many contractors are finishing and breaking up camps. Individuals fare no better. Many are returning, but a number remain hanging around the saloons in our neighborhood, now so prominently brought to the notice of the readers of the *Express.*

The casualties or accidents near Vinegaroon for the last week, as far as I have heard, may be summed up: One Murder at Vinegaroon—examination waived by A. B. Durham, charged with the murder, now committed without bail by Judge Bean, and therefore a future resident of Fort Stockton. One man shot (a Mexican) at Thomas Horan's camp. A Mr. Curran found dead and a discharged gun near him.

Lawyers at Judge Bean's are not permitted to interfere with court.

Life was cheap west of the Pecos during the time of the railroad construction. Fatal accidents as well as murders were common among the mobs of rough characters that swarmed over the roadbeds from the Pecos to Eagle Nest. Many men were buried without markers, but some graves were given wooden crosses. An expertly crafted limestone marker near the tunnel on the east side of the Pecos commemorated one of the workers. Engraved on the monument were the words ERECTED TO THE MEMORY OF JOSEPH CLULOW STONECUTTER WHO LOST HIS LIFE WHILE BATHING IN THE RIO GRANDE ON THE 6 OF AUG. 1882—AGE 23 YEARS.

The worst construction accident occurred December 12, 1882, at Dry Canyon, a short distance southeast of Vinegaroon. A large crew of men working for a subcontractor were building a two-hundred-foot-long bridge, ninety-three feet high, when the timbers of the wooden structure collapsed. Nineteen men fell with the timbers to the bottom of the canyon; eight were killed, and eleven injured. The survivors were carried out of the canyon and placed in tents in the camp on a nearby hill. A telegram was sent to Del Rio requesting that doctors be sent to the site to tend the injured. Dr. Teason, the army surgeon at Camp Del Rio, and a Dr. Nicholson arrived about three hours later. Pine coffins were made and the dead were buried in the sand and ashes of an Indian cave—the only convenient place where holes could be dug without blasting. The cave was apparently the large cave near Painted Cave section house. Two days after the accident the injured were transferred to the military hospital at Del Rio.[6]

A marker of native limestone commemorated Joseph Clulow, a stonecutter who helped build the G. H. & S. A. The inscription says he lost his life "while bathing in the Rio Grande" in 1882.

Ceremony marking the completion of the railroad, held on a bridge overlooking the Rio Grande about three miles west of the Pecos River, January 12, 1883. (Photo courtesy of Southern Pacific Lines.)

By Christmas 1882, the demand for workers on the road had decreased and wages were reduced to two dollars per day. A ceremony marking the completion of the railroad was held January 12, 1883. The *San Antonio Weekly Express* of January 18, 1883, described the occasion:

> Upper Rio Grande Tunnel No. 2, January 12: The last spike that connects the Southern Pacific and the Sunset road was driven here this afternoon with appropriate ceremonies. It took place at 2 p.m. to-day, at the east end of the second bridge, west of the mouth of the Pecos. A cedar tie was placed in position when Col. T. W. Pierce, president of the G. H. & S. A. railway company, taking a sledge, and placing a silver spike in position. . . .

The completion of the railroad was widely heralded across the nation, especially in Texas and California. The *San Francisco Daily Morning Call* front page on January 13 referred not to a silver spike but one "of wrought iron . . . very like the millions of others used in construction of the road." It was driven by Pierce "just 400 feet from the Mexican border." Pierce's speech, which eulogized the "majestic presence" of "the great canyons of the Rio Grande," invited "Divine favor upon . . . the heroic men in every department with brain and muscle who have perilled their lives in this herculean work." James Campbell, the S. P.'s assistant superintendent, drove a spike for the western crew after introducing a colorful line or two into the speechmaking: "Again," he said, "we see these men hanging over these immense lime walls suspended by ropes." A writer for the *San Antonio Daily Express* told of traveling, the day after the ceremony, on a train that was used to convey a convict work gang. He also described the section of road near the Pecos: "Down, down, down we go, sometimes on the very brink of the precipice and now crossing over deep lateral canyons on iron truss bridges and suddenly before you is a bluff too solid to cut out and is bored through by a tunnel over 1200 feet long." At one point in his travels, at the Big Canyon Bridge, one of his co-passengers "could not trust himself" to stay aboard the train and clambered down to cross the canyon on foot.

The first through freight train from the West Coast to New Orleans left San Francisco on January 25, 1883—one of the cars loaded with canned salmon and two others with barrels of port wine. Thus did ease of transportation arrive in the country west of the Pecos, initiating its settlement.

CHAPTER 4

KEEPING THE TRAINS RUNNING

The completion of the railroad was probably the most significant event that ever occurred in what would later be called Roy Bean's country. The railroad bridge across the Pecos River opened the gate to the region that had been cut off from civilization by the river's deep canyon. But keeping that gate open would not be easy.

After the final spike was driven that connected the Southern Pacific and the Galveston, Harrisburg, and San Antonio, the romance of railroad construction was gone. The drudgery of maintaining the tracks and keeping the trains running fell to dependable, hardworking men who were content to live without glamor. Section foremen sweated in the broiling summer sun and shivered in cold winter winds alongside their crews that maintained the track. Spikes that held the rails had to be kept tightly driven into the ties and a thousand other backbreaking chores had to be performed. The tracks had to be safe in order to support the coal-eating trains that snaked through the trans-Pecos at the amazing speed of thirty to thirty-five miles per hour. About every fifteen miles a railroad station was established. These stations consisted of a small depot, tool house, and quarters for the telegraph operators, section foreman, and section crew.

A typical section foreman was Simon Shaw, Sr., an Irishman who immigrated to the United States in 1881 when he was twenty-three years old. He landed in San Francisco and, after working for a short time there, joined the construction crews building the Southern Pacific. He worked under Black Jack Higgins, a foreman who directed a crew of tracklayers.

When the railroad was finished, Simon Shaw, like his friend Roy Bean, liked the area west of the Pecos and saw an opportunity for a good job. He took the job of section foreman at Painted Cave, a station located a short distance down the Rio Grande from the mouth of the Pecos. Bean meantime

Section foreman Simon Shaw (third from left) and his section crew beside their handcar at Painted Cave Depot in the Rio Grande gorge about one mile east of the Pecos River. The larger of the two signs on the depot points out that it was 1,693 miles to San Francisco, 801 miles to New Orleans. (Photo courtesy of J. P. Calk.)

Eastbound train at Painted Cave about 1884. The section foreman's residence is in the background. (Photo courtesy of J. P. Calk.)

continued running his saloon near the new depot at Eagle Nest, or Langtry as it became known.

Painted Cave Station derived its name from a huge cave in the cliff that towered above and behind the depot. The back wall of the cave displayed numerous Indian pictographs from hundreds of years before man dreamed of trains. A barrack was built by the railroad to house the section hands that worked under Shaw, although some of the men continued to live in tents. The section maintained by Shaw's crew was in the canyon formed by the Rio Grande where the railroad passed through two tunnels and numerous deep cuts. Rocks falling from the high walls of the cuts often fell on the tracks—a dangerous hazard for the trains—and a "trackwalker" was stationed at Painted Cave to watch for and remove rocks. The first man to work in this capacity under Shaw was Charlie Waits, who had come to America from Germany.

Shaw was single, so he was pleased when Mrs. Charlie Waits's sister, Anna Pater, came to Painted Cave to assist Mrs. Waits with housekeeping and cooking chores during a pregnancy. Simon was attracted to Anna and—according to the family's records—he described her as "an excellent cook and she had fine limbs." Displaying the Irish in him, he said: "Be-Jesus, there was nothing to do, no place to go, so we just walked the track after supper. I would insist that she walk the rail and in that manner I had to hold her hand." Simon and Anna were married September 19, 1888, and two of their children were born at Painted Cave. Shaw worked for the railroad for more than thirty-eight years and had four sons who later worked for the railroad.[1]

The telegraph operator at Painted Cave was George Wade, who later became general manager of the Southern Pacific. The pumper there was Bill Teasdale, who later became a conductor on the railroad and was noted for his thwarting of a bank robbery.

Even though it was a long way to any place where the men could spend their money, payday was an important time at the isolated Painted Cave station. The employees had to wait long periods for the big day to come around. A pay train, consisting of an engine, coal car, combination coach-sleeper, and the pay car carrying gold stopped at each station along the railroad to pay workers in cash. The crew consisted of a paymaster, paymaster's clerk, auditor's clerk, two guards, a cook, a porter, and the engine crew.

The pay car was a remodeled Pullman at the rear of the train. The paymaster's office had a pay window, below which was a cash till with compartments to hold $1,000 in $20, $10, and $5 gold pieces, plus a supply of silver. It took two months for the pay train to cover the Southern Pacific route, and it was not until 1888 that the practice of paying employees monthly was established.[2]

The pay train would stop in front of a depot and the workers would line up in front of the pay car. Two guards stood on the platform at the end of the pay car and as each worker at Painted Cave stepped forward to receive his money, Shaw identified the man to the roadmaster, who in turn recommended to another official that the worker be allowed to enter and receive his wages. Payment was made in gold and silver coins, and the worker left by the door at the forward end of the car with his money—carried perhaps in his cupped hands or his hat.[3]

The High Bridge

The tortuous route that the railroad followed in order to cross the Pecos River was difficult to maintain and so crooked that trains had to go very slowly for several miles. In about 1890, Jim Converse, the chief engineer of the Southern Pacific line east of El Paso, decided he could eliminate the two tunnels and shorten the railroad by eleven miles by building a bridge across the Pecos River gorge. The project required construction of a bridge 321 feet high and 2,180 feet long. It would have to be higher and more massive than any bridge ever attempted in the United States.

In March 1891, construction was begun on a new route across the Pecos, leaving the original roadbed about three miles east of Comstock, proceeding northwest to the Pecos and rejoining the old roadbed at Shumla on the west side of the river. The new roadbed to the Pecos was completed in October, and the rock piers that the wrought iron bridge would rest upon were completed in November.

James McMullen, who worked on the bridge, described the site:

> Three separate "frogtowns" sprang into existence [frogtowns were camps that "hopped along," keeping up with construction]. Although these "towns" were only 300 feet apart they might as well have been 50 miles, for you had to go either up or down if you went visiting and it was dangerous climbing.

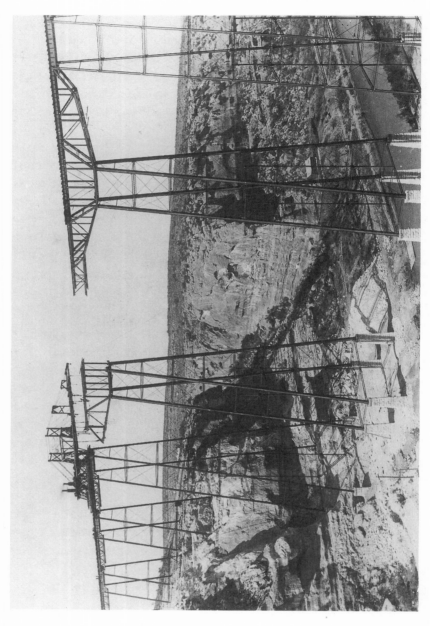

The famed Pecos River High Bridge, nearing completion in 1892. A traveler crane is placing one of the final sections atop a spindly pier. One of the thirteen saloons that operated during construction is near the river. (Photo courtesy of Center for American History, University of Texas.)

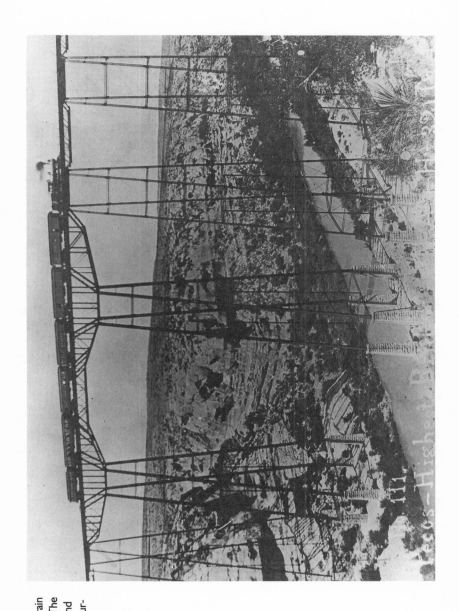

Eastbound passenger train crossing the High Bridge. The bridge was 321 feet high and 2,180 feet long. (Photo courtesy of Willie Shaw.)

There were 13 saloons around the Pecos bridge while we were building it, some on the west rim of the canyon, some on the east rim and some down in the canyon. Blaine and Sinclair had a big tent saloon with boarded sides on the east rim, and there was another operated by a man named Sikorski.

Supplies were let down from the west rim on a derrick. Torres, the justice of the peace who defeated Bean, had built a saloon and frontier amusement palace down in the canyon. [One term, Torres reportedly defeated Bean in the election for justice—and it was said that, even so, Bean refused to relinquish his position as Law West of the Pecos.] When he opened up he let 13 women over the side on the derrick, and was ready for business.

The saloon building and all of the smaller compartments were built of ocotillo stalks for walls, with brush roofs. There used to be some high old times in that place, especially around pay day. They tell me that some of the boys who lost their money quickly at faro or monte could always sneak around and peek through the ocotillo stalks and see how the rest of the crew were spending their money.[4]

Phoenix Bridge construction firm was awarded the contract to build the huge iron structure. Shortly after rails were completed to both sides of the canyon, one-half of the prefabricated bridge was unloaded on the east side of the gorge and the other half around on the west. Construction of the bridge began on the east bank of the river, a huge traveler crane being used to put the iron girders in place. When the center of the canyon was reached, the crane was dismantled and shipped by rail to the west bank, where it was again assembled and used to complete the bridge.

Work on the tall, spindly structure was dangerous and several lives were lost in the process of constructing the bridge. Each time a man was killed or drowned in the river, Judge Bean was summoned by telegraph to hold an inquest. On one occasion, seven men were killed and three others were so severely injured that there was no hope for their recovery. It was reported that Judge Bean, wanting to get back to Langtry and figuring the men would not last long, pronounced them dead and headed home.

The iron structure that would later be called High Bridge was erected in eighty-seven working days. The total cost of the iron bridge and masonry piers was $250,100. In March 1892, the new bridge—considered by many to be the eighth wonder of the world—was opened to railroad traffic. An extra fee of fifty cents was charged all passengers who were to cross the new structure, with the money designated to go to the private corporation that had been formed by railroad officials to pay for the bridge.

Trains ran over the new bridge for only two weeks when, to the astonishment of local railroaders, orders came from C. P. Huntington, president of the railroad, to abandon the new route and resume traffic over the old line. It was believed generally that Huntington held stock in the company that had been formed to build the bridge. After giving the new route a two-week trial, he became convinced that the bridge was very valuable property and consequently wanted to freeze out the remaining stockholders by abandoning the bridge. It would be of no value unless it was used by the railroad. However, in a newspaper interview in New York, Huntington gave other reasons:

> The bridge was built in order to save many miles of distance by actual mileage and equation of grades and curves against a straight line. It was a very costly bridge to build and it was not built by the Galveston, Harrisburg, and San Antonio Railroad Company, but by another Company for the reason that the parties building it could obtain money under an independent charter, when they could not if built by the Galveston, Harrisburg, and San Antonio Company. The law allows a first mortgage of only $20,000 a mile upon the road, which would be as nothing toward building a great structure like this over the Pecos. So that really the only way to build it was to do the work under an independent charter.
>
> When we commenced to use the bridge and its approaches, however, certain persons went into court in Texas to prevent the owners from receiving more than 3 cents a mile for passengers and a low rate for freight for its use, which amounted to nothing, or next to nothing, toward paying the interest on the cost of construction.
>
> After such proceedings, we of course, stopped using the bridge and went back to the old line, but I am quite satisfied that the time will come when the authorities of Texas will see the justice of allowing a charge to be made sufficient to pay fair returns on money invested.[5]

Actually, the newly formed Texas Railroad Commission had instructed the railroad that an extra fee for crossing the bridge could not be charged. The fee was dropped, and in a short period of time trains again began passing over the new bridge and the old section of railroad near the mouth of the Pecos was dismantled.

Many of the passengers were not pleased with the new bridge because they were afraid to ride across such a tall, spindly structure. At least one time the passengers had to walk across the bridge because the wind was blowing so hard up the canyon that the trainmen feared the light, wooden coaches might blow off the bridge. But the high bridge across the Pecos was safer than it looked and trains crossed it for years without serious incident. However, as the trains became heavier the bridge would sway back and forth, and it became necessary for trains to stop before crossing the bridge and then proceed very slowly in order to reduce vibration. In 1910, the bridge was reinforced and shortened 665 feet, with rock fill being placed at both ends.

The huge iron span across the Pecos had to be painted occasionally, and in 1918, Bill McBee was offered a job to help paint the high bridge for a dollar an hour. McBee, working on a ranch for twenty dollars a month, decided to get in on the big money. After the paint crew was assembled and started working, the contractor backed out on the deal and said he was going to pay six dollars a day. McBee considered that very good money in those days, so he stayed on.

The bridge contained numerous braces—immensely long bolts, about two inches in diameter. Painting the bolts took a long time and after a few days the boss told the men he would give them a day's wages for every two bolts they painted. The boss was very seldom on the job, so Bill and his partner figured out a way to paint more quickly. Bill told me in an interview:

> We dipped a tow sack [burlap bag] in the paint and then wrapped it around the bolt and covered it with another tow sack. One of us would then lock our arms around the sack and slide down the bolt, or brace. Of course if we slipped we might fall two hundred feet, because we didn't use any safety rope. We could do a full day's work in two hours that way.[6]

When the men were working near the base of the bridge, they had to walk up a long flight of steps to get out of the Pecos River canyon. The paint crew had a cable on a donkey engine that was used to hoist materials in and out of the canyon on a cable fastened to a fifty-five-gallon barrel. McBee recalled:

One day my partner and I didn't want to climb out of the canyon, so we got in the barrel and gave the donkey operator the signal to hoist up, even though it was against the rules to ride in the barrel. My partner sat down in the bottom of the barrel, but I stood up. When we started up, the barrel started spinning around and around, and oh, I was sick when we got to the top. I couldn't hardly get out of the barrel and then I couldn't stand up. The boss saw me and he knew, without being told, what had happened. Oh, he chewed me out, and he almost fired me. He didn't have to tell me not to do it again though, 'cause I had learned my lesson.

The famous Pecos High Bridge attracted its share of attention through the years. Ada Upshaw, of Langtry, and S. J. McDowell, of Del Rio, were married on the bridge in 1907, and in that same year motion picture cameramen filming a melodrama took pictures of a train chasing an automobile across the bridge. In 1921, Jimmy Doolittle, who at that time was a member of an air squadron patrolling the Mexican border, flew under the bridge in an open-cockpit airplane.

The bridge was valuable to the U.S. transportation system and it was guarded for many years. The U.S. War Department stationed troops at the bridge during the Mexican Revolution; and the Texas National Guard, the Third Infantry, the Twelfth Cavalry, and the Fifth Cavalry took turns guarding it during World War I.

J. R. Hutchins, who guarded the bridge from April 1, 1924, until World War II, lived in a frame cottage beneath the bridge. He had to climb a stairway with 252 steps in order to get out of the canyon. His furniture, supplies, and mail were lowered from the bridge to the bottom of the canyon. Trainmen would often drop newspapers and magazines to him as they passed over his home.

The Pecos bridge was heavily guarded during World War II by the Military Police, 766th Battalion. They patrolled the area around the bridge and manned antiaircraft guns to prevent it from being damaged by possible saboteurs. The rickety old High Bridge shook severely when World War II trains laden with war supplies passed over it. Finally, in 1944, the famous bridge that had served for fifty-two years was replaced by a stronger concrete-and-steel structure.

Family Life

Maintaining the railroad track was a difficult job, and as mentioned earlier, for many years section crews were stationed about every fifteen miles along the railroad. From the Pecos River westward, there were—among others—Shumla, Langtry, Osman, Pumpville, Lozier, Watkins, Thurston, Dryden, Mofeta, Feodora, and Sanderson. At each station, in the accommodations built for employees, the best and largest house always went to the section foreman and his family, the section gang members and their families crowding into two-room quarters—a bedroom and a kitchen. The foreman's family had a private outhouse; the section-gang families shared one partitioned for men and women. The yards were neat and clean and once each year railroad officials inspected every section house for cleanliness and state of repairs. Every room was inspected and an award was given to the woman in each division who had the best-kept house.

Each section foreman and his wife operated a commissary, and the arrival of the supply train, with the sacks of sugar, beans, flour, and potatoes, slabs of bacon, buckets of coffee and lard, and other staples, was a joyous time. All of the workers got their food at the commissary and were required to pay their bills each pay day. At stations like Lozier, where there was no water, the supply train also brought in water in tank cars to fill a cistern.

The section foreman was usually an Anglo; the gang members were usually Mexican Americans. English was seldom spoken, and if the section foreman's wife could not speak Spanish, she soon learned it. The section foreman worked six days a week and was required to be available on Sundays if emergencies arose. If a section foreman wanted off on a particular Sunday, he made arrangements with a neighboring foreman to cover for him. Each section foreman's house had a railroad telephone, and each morning the section foreman could get a schedule of trains from the dispatcher and thus plan the day's work on the track. Milepost signs along the railroad (Langtry was milepost 437) enabled the foreman to describe to the dispatcher where trains might encounter problems.

Railroad section foreman Simon Shaw, Jr., with his crew, maintaining S.P. tracks near Langtry. (Photo courtesy of Dorothy Shaw Billings.)

The railroading Shaw boys, Georgie, Simon, Jr., Johnnie, and Willie. All worked for the Southern Pacific Railroad—Georgie for forty-four years, Simon, Jr. for forty-six years, and Willie for forty-seven years. Johnnie was working for the S. P. when he died at age thirty-six. Their father, Simon Shaw, Sr., helped build the railroad. (Photo courtesy of Willie Shaw.)

In 1901, Simon Shaw, Sr.—by then section foreman at Pumpville—hired eighteen-year-old Allie Stidham as governess for his children. In an interview, Allie—Mrs. Allie Stidham Berry—told me about life at Pumpville in the early years of the century:

I went to Pumpville in 1901 to stay with the Shaws and teach school. Willie was the oldest, and then there was Anna, Maggie, Simon, Johnnie, Georgie, and Elizabeth (Alicia). Elizabeth was a tiny baby. I stayed there and taught a couple of years for them. During the time I was there, Emer Billings and his family and Buck Billings lived in the ranch houses across the railroad track from the Shaws.

There wasn't much recreation for us. A lot of times we would ride horseback on Sundays. Mr. Shaw had some good horses and I had my sidesaddle, so we would go horseback riding. Our main joy was to run races. There was a passenger train that came into Pumpville about ten in the mornings, so we would ride east and meet the train and then race it back to Pumpville. We could run as fast as we could and outrun the train, but after a while they would overtake us, but we would have fun racing it.

We wouldn't tell Mr. Shaw about anything like that, so one Sunday little Simon wanted to go. Well, Willie didn't want Simon to go because he figured that we couldn't run horse races with Simon along. I told Mrs. Shaw, "Let's tie a pillow behind my saddle and put Simon up there." I said, "Simon, put your arms around me and hold on and I will hold you by one leg." We would race the train, with Simon riding on the pillow behind me.

Mr. Shaw was a great one to invite men to come home and eat with him, and he was always bringing someone to the house for coffee. Mrs. Shaw was a very good cook. She always had strawberry bread and gingerbread for the men to eat. One day the conductor of the passenger train had coffee with them, and he told Mr. Shaw about running races with the kids on the horses, so for a while he wouldn't let us ride.

I had a boyfriend (we didn't call them boyfriends in those days, we called them our sweethearts or fellow). Anyway, my boyfriend came up from Sanderson, and he was going to go back on a freight train. While the train was stopped in Pumpville, this engineer got off and was talking to me. I told him, "I don't want to talk to you anymore because you are not a friend of mine." He said, "Why?" And I said, "Because you went and told Mr. Shaw about us running horse races and then for a long time he wouldn't let us ride."

He said, "Well, I'll fix that," so he told Mr. Shaw that he would slow the train down and go real slow so we could run horseback with him awhile. Well, it sounded crazy, but Mr. Shaw said, "All right."

They used to have dances at Pumpville, right across the railroad track from where we lived. Willie and Maggie loved to dance. Maggie was bashful, but she loved to dance. We had a dance there on New Year's Eve and we commenced dancing just between sundown and dark and we danced all night long—never did sit down. We had a calf barbecue and we would dance and eat.

At twelve o'clock, Buck Billings yelled out that it was midnight, so the men shot their pistols and we all yelled and hollered and stood on our heads and turned somersaults and cut up outside for a while, and finally, we all went in and danced a square dance. It was the old-time four hands around, five hands across, left and back, opposite to the right, swing to the left, get your partner, and promenade the hall. Well, the way we would promenade the hall, some of us would have a rib bone in our mouth and others might be eating a pickle, but we would dance and eat. Then we would go back out and get some more barbecue and come back in and eat. When the sun came up the next morning, we danced "Home Sweet Home." Our music was made by a fiddler and a guitar player.

Mr. Shaw loved his wife better than anything in the world and he called her Annie, me darlin'. He was a full-blooded Irishman and he used to sing Irish songs. He talked that way. He never got over that language. Soon as he would come in the house he would begin to call, "Annie, me darlin'—Annie me darlin'. . . ."

About every six weeks, Mr. and Mrs. Shaw would go to Del Rio. She wouldn't go with him until he would promise her he wouldn't get drunk. He would stay sober all the time he was in Del Rio, but he would buy a flask of whiskey and put it in his pocket to take home. He would say, "Annie, me darlin', I'm not going to get drunk. I'm just going to take a little sip." So he'd drink a little bit. Well, then sometimes by the time they got to Pumpville, he was drunk. The kids would run out to meet him, and he'd get down on his hands and knees and bray like a donkey, and the little kids would ride him to the house.[7]

Railroad Disasters

Simon Shaw and most of the other railroad men were proud of their jobs and they worked hard to make railway travel safe, but disasters did occur. *El Paso Herald* of October 28, 1899:

Another disastrous wreck is reported on the main line of the G. H. & S. A., this time 2 ½ miles east of Langtry. The accident occurred at 6:00 last evening as the fast California freight number 244 was rushing westward at the rate of 35 miles per hour. Three men, names unknown, were killed.

Suddenly and without warning the forward engine of the double header jumped the track and the rear engine and thirteen cars followed, piling and grinding in a mass of wrecked timbers and iron work. The engineer and fireman jumped for their lives and as far as reported, none were killed, though engineer Mattaire was seriously injured and at last account was unconscious, while of the two firemen, both were injured "in the back," but the exact extent of their hurts could not be learned. Neither are their names known here, as all have their homes in Del Rio, but our fireman is supposed to be Lewis Gimmel. Engineer Beatty in charge of the forward engine is supposed to have jumped and escaped uninjured.

The wrecked engines are No. 801 and 907. The train, in charge of Conductor McMullen, was on a light curve at the time of the accident and it is impossible now to know the cause of the accident. Three tramps who were stealing a ride were killed. The train was the fast California freight train loaded with miscellaneous merchandise and both the cars and their contents were total wrecks.

The Company's surgeons, Dr. Ross and Dr. Cook, went out from Del Rio to attend to the injured.

Robert T. Hill, completing the first geologic survey of the Rio Grande through the Big Bend, had concluded his boat trip from Presidio to Langtry the evening of the wreck. Soon after the members of his expedition climbed out of the river and walked up to Langtry, they heard the prolonged whistle of a locomotive, signaling distress. Hill and his nephew were asked to go with local men to assist at the site of the wreck. When he arrived at the scene, he found three severely injured hobos who had been riding in a car loaded with glass. A fourth hobo had escaped injury and Hill reported that the fellow "growled about losing his hat, and picked up some quilts and went off to sleep in the cactus."

Hill reported that looters quickly gathered at the wreck site, stealing quilts, cigars, Stetson hats, shoes, and other items. He said that Judge Roy Bean, who was at the site with his son, said, "Son, keep away"—an act of honor that forever endeared the old judge to Hill. The geologist, already exhausted from having spent twenty-two days on the Rio Grande, did not get back to the Langtry depot until three the next morning. He and his nephew threw their bedrolls on the loading platform. About three hours later, he was brusquely awakened by a railroad official, who asked him if he was the hobo who had escaped from the wrecks.[8]

Judge Bean's behavior at train wrecks was not always as gentlemanly as that described by Hill. Mrs. Farley, some of whose reminiscences have been given earlier in this book, told of Bean's activity at another wreck:

> There was a train wreck on Osman Canyon, west of Langtry—this was while we were living on the Pecos in about 1897—and Papa went out there. He said Judge Roy Bean was there with a Mexican and they had a *carretilla* with a burro hitched to it. Papa said Roy Bean and the Mexican were shoveling this sugar up and putting it in the cart. The judge got off with a lot of sugar there. This car ran off the bridge and spilled a lot of sugar, and that's why they later called it Sugar Bridge.[9]

Probably the most disastrous train wreck that ever occurred west of the Pecos was at Maxon Station, west of Sanderson, on the night of March 6, 1902. Willie Shaw told me that story:

> The wreck occurred about three miles east of Maxon on a ten-degree curve of the railroad. In those days they had eighteen-mile-per-hour speed limits on the curves, but that engineer had left Sanderson and he had lost some time going down, so they notified him they wanted him to make up some time. I don't know how certain it is, but I heard that when he left Sanderson, he said, "Well, by God, I'll give them a ride tonight that they will never forgot."
>
> Joe Powers, he was my clerk for years, he was in that wreck. He was riding in the train and he and just a few more got out. All of the train but the back end burned up. There were two or three car loads of Italian people that all burned up and of course there were other cars with women, children, and men burning up.
>
> The only way they could notify anyone about the wreck was to walk to Maxon, so some of the men walked to Maxon and the railroad men there got the word out about the wreck.
>
> I don't know how many people were killed in the Maxon wreck. Of course, they had the small coaches in them days and they only carried about thirty people in each car.[10]

Newspaper accounts of the wreck reveal that it was believed that thirty-eight people perished in the accident. Some of the passengers thought that the train was traveling at least seventy miles per hour at the time of the accident.

Railroad Robbers

In the early days of railroading, three types of disasters were expected to occur occasionally—train wrecks, train robberies, and bridges washing away. The railroad experienced all three kinds of disasters in the country west of the Pecos.

The first recorded train robbery in Roy Bean country occurred September 2, 1891, near Dryden. The robbers reportedly escaped with $50,000 and a call immediately was made for assistance from the Texas Rangers. Ranger Captain Frank Jones, of Company D, was dispatched in pursuit of the robbers. Three months later, he wrote the following account of the chase in a letter to a friend, Mrs. Pauline Baker, of Uvalde, Texas:

When I left Uvalde went straight to El Paso as an attached witness for the Federal grand jury then in session. Before reaching El Paso received a telegram, forwarded from Alpine, stating that the robbers were in camp about 50 miles from Comstock, a station on the Southern Pacific road, and about 30 miles west of Del Rio. I went on to El Paso that evening and the next day saw the Division Supt. and made arrangements for transporting men and horses from Alpine to Comstock.

The next day I came down on the passenger train to Alpine and got off and came out to camp and got the men and horses and returned to Alpine the same evening. We boarded a freight train about nine o'clock in the night and reached Comstock about noon the next day. Here we left the railroad and that night camped at old "Camp Hudson" on Devils River. The next day we arrived at the place these robbers had camped and slaughtered a beef, but they had been gone 3 days.

The next day I followed their trail across the country about 40 miles and camped without water for our horses, but found sufficient in some rocks for our own use. The next day the trail led in the direction of the Pecos and we came to a ranch at "Howard's

Well," an old time station on the old overland stage line from San Antonio to El Paso. At this point some parties had seen the men we were following and they were yet 3 days ahead of us. A few miles from this place we again found their trail and followed it all that day. The next morning we heard of them and they were only one day ahead of us, they having laid up 2 days to rest their horses. We would have overtaken them the next day, but they did not ride close together and the grass was almost knee high and we had some difficulty in trailing them.

The next day about noon we followed their trail to a ranch where I expected to find them as the sign was quite fresh. We ran up to the house and surrounded it and found no one there but a lady and she was so frightened she could hardly talk. She was a Northern woman. After she got breath enough to talk she informed me that the robbers had been gone about 4 hours and that a young man who worked for them had ridden off with them. Said they wanted him to purchase some horses and as this young man had some for sale they had gone up the next pasture where they could catch them in.

I pushed on and on reaching this place found 2 of the robbers' broken horses near the pen, and of course, I then knew two of them had a fresh mount. It was now about 2 o'clock and we had ridden very hard that day and had no dinner. We unpacked and while the boys were getting dinner a man came up and he proved to be the man who had left the ranch with the robbers that morning. On being questioned he said that he had sold them two splendid young horses and that they were in camp only one mile from us. He said that he ate dinner with them and they had a splendid place in which to make a fight. He described them so accurately that I knew positively the two who had obtained the new horses; they were John Flynt and Jack Wellington, the worst men by far in the party.

We hurried through dinner and packed up and went straight to their camp. I had fully made up my mind to go on them no matter when or how I found them. They must have started about the same time we did for when I reached the place they had camped for noon we saw them about one mile ahead riding along very leisurely. I noticed that they were making a curve to the left and I quit the road and went up the bed of a dry ravine and quartering with them. When we came out of this ravine they were in plain view and distant about half a mile.

We increased our gait to a brisk trot and when about 300 yards from them I ordered a charge at them and we went with our guns drawn. They did not see us until their horses shied at the noise ours made running. Lansford did not attempt to escape but the others put spurs to their horses and the chase was on in good earnest. Flint and Wellington staid together and I followed them about 3 miles when Wellington's horse was shot and could not run any more. Wellington jumped off and gun in hand started to some rocks on the side of the mountain. When he dismounted I was sure that Flynt would too and that they would fight to the death. I dismounted and shot at Wellington 3 times but it was a long distance and I undershot him. He had a much better gun than mine, it being a large long range rifle with cartridges as long as your finger. I knew that he was a famous shot and at long range had a decided advantage.

I remounted my horse and ran up to about 100 yards of him where I felt pretty sure I could kill him the first shot. I then called out to him that I was an officer and did not wish to hurt him and he surrendered. In the meantime, Flynt ran on and the two men who were next to me I sent on after him telling them to follow him until they ran him into some hole and that as soon as I captured or killed Wellington I would follow on.

There had been so much talk about Wellington that I was anxious to try conclusions with him and I guess we would have had a regular Winchester duel only he saw some of the men coming on up the flat and knew that in case he killed me he could not get away with his life. He was not a particle unnerved.

Flynt ran about 5 miles farther on then dismounted and went into a ravine in a little thicket, and after making a note in his pocket book as to what disposition was to be made of his property, blew his brains out. Some time in the chase he had been shot through the body, but I do not think the wound was necessarily a fatal one. You who understand anatomy would be a better judge of that than I am. The ball entered just under the right shoulder blade making its exit through the right nipple. He had not bled a great deal except from the wound in the head. He had not bled a particle from the mouth or nose. We procured a hack and brought his body to a ranch 8 miles from where he was killed. The next day we buried him the best we could under the circumstances, the prisoners assisting us. I had to purchase the partition out of a house to get lumber to make a coffin for him. Flynt was a young man who had been given good advantages, but gambling and drinking had ruined him. He was to have been married in Oct. but got into this trouble. I had met the girl a few times and she is a very bright woman. Since his death she "cut me dead" but I am under the impression that I will survive. I am really sorry for her.

I would give almost anything to know the history of this man Wellington. He is a gentleman and he is a very handsome man. Has fine blue eyes, fair complexion, blond hair and mustache. He said that he and Flynt had put up several jobs to get to kill me. But enough of train robbers . . . . [11]

Another train robbery occurred in 1897 at Lozier Canyon, about ten miles west of Pumpville. For several miles, the railroad track went up Lozier Canyon, and the railroad station called Lozier was located on a big flat area on the eastern side of the canyon. Lozier, like other stations along the railroad, consisted of a depot, shipping pens, and houses where the section foreman, operators, and section crew lived. It was a rather isolated site—a logical place for train robbers to choose. Simon Shaw, Sr. was section foreman at the time of the robbery and Addie Upson was the day operator. A Miss Frink was the night operator.

One night, two men entered the depot and told Miss Frink that they wanted to catch the westbound passenger train that would be coming through Lozier. Miss Frink explained to the men that the passenger train always stopped at Lozier, but the men insisted that they had to catch the train and told her to be sure and flag down the train if it looked like it was not going to stop.

As usual, the train stopped at Lozier and took on water for the steam locomotive. The two passengers got on the train and, huffing and puffing its clouds of steam, the train began to roll westward again. Just a short distance west of Lozier station, one of the two men moved forward along the slowly moving train and appeared in the engine. He pulled a pistol on the engineer and fireman and made them stop the train. Meanwhile, the other man held a gun on the conductor and porter and made them uncouple the train just behind the baggage car, which was immediately back of the engine and coal car. The robbers then directed the engineer and fireman to pull the baggage car on up the track to a place where four other men on horses were waiting.

While the trainmen were held at gunpoint, the robbers ripped open mail sacks in a hurried search for money. They found several cloth bags full of Mexican money, which they considered practically worthless, and threw them out the door of the baggage car. The sacks struck sharp boulders along the edge of the canyon and broke open, scattering Mexican coins among the rocks.

The roadmaster was on the train, and as soon as he realized what was going on, he ran all the way back to the Lozier station and woke up Shaw and his crew of section hands. The men did not have guns, so they gathered up pick handles and bars used for track maintenance and started out for the robbery scene. Walking briskly along the tracks, they heard an explosion, caused by the bandits attempting to blow up a safe in the baggage car, and decided they had better not challenge the robbers.

The robbers—later reported to be the notorious Black Jack Ketchum and his gang—escaped on horseback. Ranger Captain John R. Hughes and some of his men, who arrived by train from Ysleta the next day to take up the trail of the robbers, were unsuccessful in finding either the men or the stolen money.

A few years later, two other men who attempted to hold up a train in the same vicinity were not so fortunate. On the afternoon of March 12, 1912, a man entered the W. H. Dodd Mercantile Store at Langtry and talked with storekeeper Dodd, who also had a roominghouse, making a deal with him for a room for the night; he then tried to pay for the room. Dodd told the man that he did not need the money in advance and told the fellow he could pay for the room the next day. The man replied that he might have to get up pretty early in the morning and he did not want to disturb anyone, so Dodd accepted the money in advance.

Cross Dodd, son of W. H., told me more of the story in an interview:

> The man hung around the store that evening and was a likable fellow. He wasn't a forward person, but was friendly and was the

sort of a man that you kinda liked. While he was in the store that evening, a couple of Mexican kids came into the store to get something, and they were barefooted. This fellow told my Daddy, he said, "Mr. Dodd, put some shoes and stockings on those children for me, will you? I'll pay for it."

The stranger and my dad put the stockings and shoes on the kids and this fellow paid Dad for them. Of course, the kids were tickled to death.

The next morning this fellow caught the train and he joined up with his partner, and they tried to hold up the train up toward Dryden, and the fellow that stayed with us was killed.[12]

The two slain robbers were Ben Kilpatrick and Ed Welch. It is not known which of the two spent the night of March 12, 1912, at Langtry. Kilpatrick, a notorious outlaw and train robber, was known over much of the United States as the Tall Texan. He had been a member of the Wild Bunch and the High-Five Gang, train-robbing gangs that at one time or another had consisted of such characters as Kid Curry, Will Carver, Tom (Black Jack) Ketchum, Harry Longbaugh (the Sundance Kid), Butch Cassidy, and Kilpatrick's long-time girlfriend, Laura Bullion.

Kilpatrick had participated in the robbery of a Great Northern train in 1901; in attemtping to rob the Southern Pacific train near Dryden, he chose to use the same method as that used earlier. On the night of March 13, 1912, S.P. passenger train Number 9 was chugging westward toward Sanderson and had just passed Mofeta siding when Kilpatrick appeared in the engine. He held a pistol on the engineer and fireman and ordered them to stop on a big bridge just ahead. As the train stopped, the conductor, named Urkel, and the porter, Ed Simmon, stepped out to see what the trouble was. Kilpatrick jabbed Simmons, a black, in the stomach with a rifle and told him to uncouple the train just in front of the passenger cars.

The *San Antonio Weekly Express* of March 15, 1912, gives the story of the robbery as told by David Trousdale, who was an express messenger on the train:

One of the men got on the engine at Dryden, although I did not know this until the train came to a stop on the railroad line. But a minute or two thereafter the Negro porter came to the door of the car and called me. I recognized his voice. Just about that time I was finishing up my work before reaching Sanderson. The Negro porter said: 'They's some robbers out here. You better git out.' As I opened the door, I looked down the barrel of a gun one of the robbers was holding on me. I got out of the car.

Shortly after getting out of the car, I asked both the conductor and porter if either of them had a gun. Right after that the robbers put me on the engine. The mail and baggage and express car had been cut off and I guess we ran along for a half a mile or a mile.

Just as soon as we came to a stop, or shortly before we came to a stop, the engineer blew the whistle of the locomotive four times. It was as I learned later, the signal of the big man [Kilpatrick] to his partner that everything was all right. They were not going to rob the train if there were any soldiers on board. Well, the big fellow went into the cars and the other remained on the outside. In the mail car he got hold of five pouches and one of these was cut open, the man seeing some registered letters, threw these back into the pouch with the intention of getting them later on.

There were only two express packages removed. One of these was valued at $2 and the other at $34. So you see there was not a great deal obtained by the robber who was doing the work. But you know, this fellow was making me madder all of the time. If I was not holding my hands high enough he seemed to take delight in jabbing me in the side with his gun. However, I kept jollying him along and when he got into that section of the car where the express packages were stacked he broke open a few of these. It was while he was doing this that I wondered how to kill him. I was mad for I was determined I would have it out with him for jabbing me in the side and bruising me up. I'd have fought him with my fists had it come to that.

Well, in going through the car I saw a maul lying on top of the barrel of oysters. These mauls are built something like a croquet mallet, only the handle is about as thick as the handle of a hatchet. I decided then that if I could get him in the right position I could hit him with the maul. You know, you can hit an awful blow with such a maul. Why, I've broken up a box of ice at a blow. To make the story short, I kept on jollying him along. After a while I got his confidence and could lay my hands on him. I helped him along. Then I showed him packages I said he had never seen before.

He was looking over these packages in a stooped sort of position and as quietly as I could I lifted the maul from the top of the oyster barrel and he did not detect me. While he was stooping over I struck him at the base of the skull.

The first blow broke the man's neck. As he went down in a heap, a light groan came from him. He never spoke. I struck him a second and third time. On the third blow the maul crashed through his skull and the man's brains spattered over the side of the car. After I saw he was done for, I took two Colt pistols from his body. One of these I later gave to the mail clerk and the other one I gave to my helper. I kept the man's Winchester. When the robber fell, he landed on top of a stack of packages. In some of these there was some glass and this was broken by his weight.

About the first thing I did after that was to find the gas key and turn out the lights in the car. Then I waited for some time. Nothing developed, so I decided to fire a shot through the roof of the car to attract attention. Then I took up my position about midway of the car, there being one door still open, and that was the one where the porter first called. The lights of the combination car were shining through the end doors of the cars and had the robber entered through the other car I could have seen him and had he come in the door of my car I would still have gotten a bead on him.

After firing the shot I did not have to wait long, I soon heard the other robber on the outside of the car lying low and pretty soon he was calling for Frank [the other robber]. Pretty soon I saw a head poked out from back of some baggage. I could not get a bead on him at once, and so I waited for a little while. It wasn't long, I saw his head again and I cut down on him. The bullet struck him about an inch above the left eye. It passed through his skull and then passed out through the car. There was just two shots fired, the first to attract attention and the other was used with deadly effect on the second robber, who was the smaller of the two. It was with the first robber's gun that I killed the second man. The rifle is 401 caliber of 1910 model.

From the two men I got four pistols and two rifles. One of the pistols I brought back with me and the officials at Sanderson told me I would be given the rifle with which I killed the second man . . . .

The first man I killed was six feet one inch in height and weighed 210 pounds, and the other man, who was always addressed as 'partner,' was baldheaded, of medium stature and, I would say, weighed about 160 or 165 pounds. 'Partner' seemed to be the man who directed the operations. It was the big fellow who looked to me to be green at the game. I jollied him a lot and frequently complimented him on his work and the manner in which he went about it. Among other things I gave him to understand that the company did not pay me to protect its property. It was just by jollying him that I got the drop on him.

At the time I killed the first man the mail clerk was in the combination car and my helper was about ten or twelve feet from me in my car. At the time none of us had guns on us. My shotgun and pistol were in my desk and then when I laid for the second man I decided I would use the first robbers rifle because I could work that faster than the shotgun I had in the car. After a while the fireman came back to the car and asked me to open the door. I told him I had killed two men, and told him to go back and get the conductor and some passengers. When he first called I believed there might be some more robbers on the outside with him who were making him talk. So after a while he and the conductor and probably fifteen passengers came back to the car . . . .

There were some who believed more than two men were concerned in the holdup. I could not come to that belief after it was all over. There were a couple of hoboes on the oil tank of the engine. One of these was a man with a wooden leg and the other seemed to be a young fellow. Both of the hoboes remained on the oil tank throughout the incident. Possibly they might have gotten off after the train was again coupled up. Their walking away might have started the rumor that others were concerned in the robbery.

The *Express* story continued with the U.S. Mail clerk's story. He concluded: "I shudder when I think of what our finish might have been had Trousdale's shot hit dynamite and nitroglycerin on the robber's person instead of tearing the top of his head off. . . . Too much can not be said of Trousdale's nerve and bravery . . . while we were being marched from the cab of the engine he whispered to me: 'These outlaws are green, and we'll await our chance and get them, sure.'"

The bodies of Ben Kilpatrick and Frank Hobeck were prominently displayed at Sanderson and photographs of the dead men were widely published in newspapers across Texas. Train robbers apparently got the message: this was the last train robbery in the area.

Floods

Floods also caused problems for the railroad. Even though the country west of the Pecos was usually dry, heavy rains did occur occasionally. The rainwater ran rapidly off the rocky hills, and the normally dry draws and canyons flowed like rivers. Willie Shaw told me about one of these floods:

> I was section foreman at Osman in 1919. It started raining one evening and it rained and it rained. In them days we had one of those high gauges, you know. It had an eight-inch cylinder on top with a copper pipe that went down through the middle. It was about two and a half feet high, as well as I remember.
>
> It poured rain all night long. So, when I got up, Osman Draw was running and I went west on my handcar to the section about a mile and a half west of Osman. Everything was alright up there. There was a bridge over Osman there and water was almost up to the top of it.
>
> I came on back to the house and I called Mister Cole, the dispatcher. I said, "Mister Cole, we had an awful rain here last night and it is still raining and the creek is very high." I said, "The siding is washed out here at Osman and it is undermining the telephone where I am calling from."
>
> About that time one of the bridges across Osman washed out, and it washed down the creek and hit another one and tore down the telegraph line, and the bridge went out just about the time I was talking to him.
>
> Mister Cole called up the operator at Langtry and said, "Get somebody down to Osman right quick. I was talking to Willie, and

he said the telephone was undermining and then the line went out." He thought the telephone booth had washed down the canyon.

I put the handcar on and went on down the track and the first big bridge east of Osman was all right. It was about a quarter of a mile long. But, from there on I had nineteen big bridges washed out.

That morning I checked the rain gauge, and there was twenty-three inches of rain that night. On that big gauge, every tube that you emptied out of that was an inch of rain and I emptied out twenty-three times.

The railroad was tied up and they brought in repair gangs all the way from California and all the way from Houston, but it took nineteen days to get the railroad open.

There was a big bridge west of Bean Siding that was about four hundred feet long and there was a big one east of Bean about six hundred feet long. They had an oak deck, you know, and by golly the bridge right west of Bean broke the rail right on the west end and that bridge turned over and over and wrapped around and formed a chain of the rail there for almost a quarter of a mile. Every bridge on down the canyon washed away. Oh, that was a mess!"[13]

The railroad crossed Osman Canyon several times, and washouts in the canyon were such a problem that in 1927, the Southern Pacific constructed a shortcut through the hills north of the canyon. This shortened their route and eliminated the problem of the bridges washing away on Osman Canyon.

Despite floods, robberies, and wrecks, the railroad prospered. Business was brisk in the country west of the Pecos: pens for livestock at the railroad stations were hubs of activity and ranchers drove cattle, horses, sheep, and goats to the pens and loaded them for shipment to livestock markets.

The railroad played an important part indeed in the development of Roy Bean country. One old timer, referring to all the houses, pens and fence posts in the area made of railroad ties, said the railroad contributed much more to the country than its officials ever realized.

CHAPTER 5

SQUATTING AND HOMESTEADING

With the Indians driven from the trans-Pecos and the trains puffing through the region, the vast area of canyons and rocky hills was becoming tolerable as a place where families could live. By 1882, much of the rest of Texas had become pretty well settled. Hardy souls with the pioneer spirit were looking for new places to go. Outlaws and desperadoes were getting hemmed in by the law in the so-called civilized areas, and they, too, were looking for new places—and the rough country west of the Pecos still had lots of isolated terrain in which to hide. It was also short on law. Roy Bean was the Law West of the Pecos, but he was no angel, and he was too smart to snoop into a stranger's affairs.

A lot of people admired the scenery west of the Pecos as they peered from their coaches through the black smoke that spewed from the train engines. Most of the few people who got off the train to investigate the possibilities of living in the area realized in a hurry that it would take more effort and sacrifice to live west of the Pecos than it was worth; and most of the people who chose to stay were those not accustomed to the luxuries of society. As a rule, they were those who liked to enjoy nature without too many folks around.

From the following accounts, we can piece together a sense of what life was like for Roy Bean and these hardy settlers. Before 1900, the country between the lower stretches of the Pecos River and the Rio Grande was mostly wide open to those who wanted to use it. If the land did not have a spring, river front, or a permanent pothole (a hole or depression in the rocky bed of a canyon that would hold water), it was virtually worthless.

The first settlers who brought cattle, mules, horses, and sheep westward did not have an easy task. It was a constant struggle to get the wagons and stock across the many canyons, and water was scarce. The days of summer were often awfully hot. The sheep, cattle, and goats were hard to drive in the summer because they tried to hide their heads in the shade of the bushes. Horses could not be ridden for long without shoes, because the rocks wore their hooves down until they became sore, or in the ranchers' words, tenderfooted.

The settlers had to locate where there was water. Their choices were limited to spots on the Pecos and Rio Grande where trails could be worked down the bluffs to the river, or to the few springs in the region, or to potholes that caught enough rainwater to be dependable. But no matter where people settled, there was usually a water problem of some sort. If they lived along the Pecos, the water was salty; on the Rio Grande, it was usually so muddy that it had to settle in a bucket for a few hours. Most of the springs in the region were in the bottom of deep canyons. If the settlers lived near potholes, their water was often stagnant, and there might not be any water during periods of drought.

If trails could not be worked to water in the rivers or to potholes in the deep canyons, some of the pioneers rigged up "waterworks"—systems whereby buckets of water could be pulled to the top of the bluffs. One such system, on the Pecos, was arranged so that buckets of water could be pulled from the river to the top of a three-hundred-foot cliff. A tower about twelve feet high with four wooden legs was anchored to solid rock a few feet back from the top of the cliff. A small cable was fastened to a large bolt anchored into the solid rock a few feet back from the tower, and the cable then ran over the tower and off the bluff. The other end of the cable was fastened to another large bolt secured at water level at the base of a cliff on the opposite side of the river, the cable swinging freely between the tower and the water. To get water from the river, a bucket attached to a pulley on the cable was tied to a long rope that was used to lower the bucket to the river. When the bucket struck the bluff at the water's edge, the bucket tilted enough to fill with water. The rancher then cranked a large wooden winch that wound the rope around a drum and pulled the bucket to the top of the cliff, the water then being emptied into a pothole in a small arroyo a few feet away. The pothole had been enlarged by the addition of a concrete dam, about two feet high and six feet long.

Using such systems to water sheep and cattle and provide a few buckets of brackish water for camp took a lot of work; thus, instead of using winches, some of the waterworks in Roy Bean country were operated by tying the rope to the horn of a saddle and using horsepower to raise the buckets.

From a variety of sources (land abstracts, local history, hearsay, and so on), we know the names of a number of ranchers active in the Langtry country before 1900. They included Roy Bean, Cesario and Jesus Torres, Marcus Ocejo, John Billings and sons Buck and Emer, Joe Burdwell, George Upshaw, Bill Ike Babb, W. H. Dodd, Henry Roach, Zeno Fielder, Ed Ramsey, H. C. Tardy, John F. Camp, Henry Morehead, and the Pecos Land and Cattle Company, headquartered at Myers Springs, which was owned by people in Massachusetts.

Bernardo Torres, of Fort Stockton, was granted the land where the town of Langtry was later established. He died in 1882 and his widow sold the land to Bernardo's brother, Cesario. Cesario did not move to Langtry but sent his son Jesus there to manage the property. Jesus ranched for a short time and then opened a store and saloon at Langtry.

The Pecos Land and Cattle Company owned 106 alternate sections in the Dryden-Pumpville area and leased or used a further amount of land of equal size. Some of their leased land at Myers Springs and Cedar Springs belonged to the aforementioned cavalry officer, John L. Bullis. In 1885, W. W. Simonds replaced a man named Lugee as manager of the ranch, and Daniel Franks was hired as foreman of stock. In 1890, John M. Doak—whose book about ranch life will be mentioned later—became foreman of the Pecos Land and Cattle Company. Doak held the position until the ranch was sold in 1895 to Dominick Hart.

John Billings came to the Langtry country in 1884 with herds of cattle and horses. He headquartered his ranching operations at Pumpville and ran more than two thousand head of cows bearing his thirty-three half-circle brand on the open range between the Pecos, Rio Grande, and Lozier Canyon. Billings and his wife and younger children lived in a dugout at Langtry during the school term, so the youngsters could attend school there. His older sons, Emer and Buck, stayed at Pumpville in the house there, when they were not camped on the range. Billings, too, later sold out to Dominick Hart.

Of other ranchers, we know that Tardy brought a herd of cattle to the Langtry area in 1885 and turned them loose on the range northwest of town. His foreman was George Burrow. At that time the country was overstocked with horses and they sold for three dollars a head. Ocejo, a native of Spain, came to the United States in 1871 and by 1900, was ranching on the Pecos about six miles northeast of Langtry; Roach had a small ranch on Antonio Creek, west of Langtry, where he dammed up a small spring, built a rock pen nearby, and is known to have been living there in 1885; Zeno Fielder moved to the Langtry area from Mazatlán, Mexico, and ranched north of town. He built a house in Langtry and served as postmaster after Jesus Torres moved away.

Ramsey was ranching west of Langtry in 1888. He built a house near the spring just above where Ramsey Draw ran into the Rio Grande. In 1941, I found parts of a coffin protruding from an eroded bank near Ramsey Spring and my father, Guy Skiles—some of whose memories have already been recorded in this book—told me that Ramsey had buried a child while they lived there.

Morehead ranched at the mouth of the Pecos, and was mentioned by John Doak in the book he coauthored with R. J. Lauderdale, *Life on the Range and on the Trail*. Doak, writing about crossing the Pecos just above its confluence with the Rio Grande in 1885, chronicled:

> We found the Pecos at high water and had to swim the herd of cattle and saddle horses. At the crossing there lived only one family—Mr. Morehead, his wife, and daughter, Patty. . . . Mr. Morehead had a skiff, so he took all our provisions and bedding across; then we took the bed of the chuck wagon and put it on the skiff; which he also took across. We tied the rocking-bolster and the king-bolt for the wagon frame, so it could not come apart in the water, held the tongue of the wagon, and dragged the whole thing across the river. We had luck and did not lose a thing.[1]

William Henry Dodd, a native of Birmingham, England, was another of those on the Pecos. He emigrated to the United States in 1886 and began ranching about fifteen miles north of Langtry in 1888, in partnership with John Ashby. He and his wife lived on the Pecos until 1896, when he moved to Langtry.

Bill Ike Babb—about whom we hear more later—moved livestock to the Pecos River in 1898 and leased Pecos County school land. By 1915, he owned 105 sections of land. His son, John, homesteaded adjoining land on the Pecos, and another son, Will, bought land on the Pecos a few miles upstream from its confluence with the Rio Grande.

Dominick Hart, whose name is mentioned above, bought a large tract of land from the Pecos Land and Cattle Company in 1895 for twenty-seven cents an acre and established ranching headquarters about five miles north of Pumpville. In 1907, he controlled more than a thousand sections (640,000 acres) of land. In 1916, Hart sold 374 sections of land north of the railroad to Sidney Webb and sold his land south of the tracks to Hal Hamilton and Jim White. J. M. Bassett purchased the land Webb had bought from Hart and ranched if for several years. His brand was the block-Y.

A more detailed account of life at this time was given to me by Beula Burdwell Farley in an interview:

> My folks came out here in 1895, and landed at Pandale Crossing on March fifteenth, where there were lots of trees on this side of the river—and that's where we camped. We camped at the mouth of Fielder Canyon, and had a wagon and cows and horses.
>
> I don't remember exactly when the Babbs came in there, but they camped there near us; they were coming from Coleman. It was probably several months after we got there. And then the Upshaws came along.
>
> Every time there was a new baby, Mama and Papa would start out in a wagon to a doctor. They would take all of us, and when Robert was born, they took us to Eagle Pass. And then in a couple of years they started again, and they got down to Horsehoe Bend near Comstock, and Lillie was born in the wagon. She was the eleventh child, and Mama had two orphans, her sister's child and my sister's child.
>
> We moved up on the Rio Grande May 1, 1900, about three miles above Langtry. When we lived there; there was Ambrose, Ed, Jim, and myself going to school. The next year Robert was added, and the next year Johnny, the orphan boy, started to school.[2]

Bill Ike Babb and his wife settled on the Pecos a few miles below the mouth of Howard Draw. Mrs. Myrtle Babb Cash, one of the Babb children, told of living there:

> Papa built a picket house. He cut straight cedar poles, peeled the bark off them and stood them up together in a ditch to make what we called a picket wall. He chinked up the cracks between the

Cowboys on the Babb Ranch circa 1913. Left to right are George Brown, Jesus Vásquez (cook), Bill Ike Babb, French Ingram, John Netherland, Buster Babb, John Babb, and Boye Babb. (Photo courtesy of Myrtle Babb Cash.)

Roy Cash, Bill Ike Babb, and Alex Powell at the Babb home, north of Langtry. Smokehouse is at right. (Photo courtesy of Myrtle Babb Cash.)

cedar poles with mud. Papa hauled in sacahuista [a grass-like plant of the yucca family] from up on Howard Draw and tied it into bundles with dagger leaves, and put it on top of the house for the roof. The house had two rooms and a hall and a front porch—and of course it had dirt floors.

A big flood on the Pecos came and washed almost all of our things away—horses, wagons, and most of our things. We didn't stay there but about six months and then we moved. Some of the family had chills and fever, and the doctor in Del Rio said it was too wet, and that caused the chills and fevers.[3]

While the Babbs lived in the cedar and sacahuista house on the river, Mr. Babb and the older boys were away from home one time, and Mrs. Babb was at home with the children: Maudie, about fifteen years old; Rosa, thirteen; Myrtle, three; Dillard, about two; and Walter, who was a small baby. During the night, Mrs. Babb got up to tend to Walter and as she walked about on the dirt floor a rattlesnake bit her on the foot.

Mrs. Babb and the older girls killed the snake and lanced the place where Mrs. Babb had been bitten. Mrs. Babb told Rosa to go to the nearest neighbor's for help. Rosa saddled up a horse and started out in the middle of the night, heading up the river toward the Netherlands' house. She had to cross the river twice and ride several miles in the darkness through rough brush country. As soon as Rosa reached the Netherlands', Mrs. Netherland rode back with her to help treat the snakebite. They killed a chicken, cut it open, and put Mrs. Babb's foot into the carcass so that the warm body would draw out some of the poison. Next they put black, crysillic salve, which was often used as a worm medicine, on the bite. After other remedies had also been tried, Mrs. Babb was given whiskey until she could feel no pain.

Bill Ike Babb and son Will were camped on Havensilla Draw. At daylight, one of the children was sent after them. When Babb got home, he sent Will to Juno to get a doctor, but by the time the doctor arrived there was little left for him to do: he provided additional treatment to Mrs. Babb and scolded the others for giving whiskey to a snakebite victim. The helpers never knew which of the remedies was most beneficial, but Mrs. Babb soon recovered.[4]

Shelter West of the Pecos

Prior to 1900, very little lumber was used in the trans-Pecos ranch country. Some of the folks who settled along the rivers were fortunate, finding caves in the bluffs to protect them from the weather. Others near the river used trees from along the river to build shelters: willow limbs were straight and suitable for building crude houses, and river-cane, often used for walls, was also laid across poles to provide a roof.

Folks ranching in the hills, away from a river, lived in dugouts built into the hillsides. Cedar limbs, serving as rafters, were covered with bear grass, lechuguilla, or sotol. Caliche, a local limestone residue, placed on the roof held it down and helped keep out the rain and wind. In most places, it was too rocky to dig very far into the hillsides, so the front portion of the dugout often would have walls made of stacked rocks. It was unusual for an early settler to have a house that consisted of more than two rooms; however, a big arbor or two usually served as part of the living quarters. In the mild climate, most of the living was done under the arbor. A few early settlers lived in tents, but tents were expensive and few settlers had much money for things other than livestock, which might make them a little money. A house, of whatever sort, was usually more comfortable than a tent.

Another versatile natural building material was ocotillo. When braced against heavier limbs, the spindly, thorny, ocotillo limbs served as walls and roofs. It also was used in making corrals for sheep and goats. Sotol houses, too, were common. These were made by putting up posts four or five feet apart where the walls were needed and then fastening the sotol bloom stalks to the posts. After the sotol stalks were tied in place, one on top of the other on both sides of the posts, the space of three or four inches between the layers of stalks was then filled with small rocks.

Other than the expensive lumber shipped out on the train from San Antonio or Del Rio, the most abundant construction material not gathered from the region was—as noted at the end of the preceding chapter—railroad crossties, commonly referred to simply as ties. The wood-craving inhabitants of the region kept a close watch on railroad activities and were always on the lookout for ties that had been discarded or that were not carefully watched by the railroad employees. Many section foremen were cooperative and informed their needy friends of the location of discarded ties. The ties were used to build houses and barns, for fence posts, and to keep woodstoves burning.

Houses made of ties were generally built in log-cabin fashion, with the ties stacked together like logs. In some instances, the ties were stood on end in a trench; when securely tamped into position, the row of ties formed a stout wall. Cracks between ties were chinked with mud or concrete. After the walls were built, poles would be placed across the top and covered with dirt to form a roof. Caliche was often brought in, moistened, and packed for the floor.

Some of the dugouts had roofs made of railroad ties. The ties would be laid across the top of the dugout, mud would be placed between the ties, and a seal of dirt piled on top. One such house was at Watkins, a railroad siding. The dugout went back into the side of a caliche hill. Dirt and caliche dug out of the side of the hill were used to cover the ties on the roof.

Railroad ties were excellent for making strong corrals, and when the country was fenced, they were used as fence posts. Since it was so hard to dig postholes in this rocky country, the railroad ties were often split to form two posts so that the post holes would not have to be so big.

Any kind of lumber could be used in building houses and if it was free, so much the better. A one-room house north of Langtry (said to have been built by Roy Bean's son Sam) was partially built of beer barrel staves. They curved, of course, and the slightly tapered boards did not fit together very well, but they were better than nothing, and were inexpensive. Maybe Sam figured that using beer barrels for building a house was justification enough for having to empty the barrels.

After some of the settlers established ranches and were able to afford good, permanent houses, they chose to build of rock. Rock was plentiful and cost nothing, but cement to hold it together was expensive. Henry Mills told me how his family made lime to build their rock house:

When I was a big kid, Papa wanted to build a rock house at Pandale. Cement cost a lot of money in those days, so he decided to make his own lime.

Up the creek above the house, there was a big caliche bluff that he thought would be a good place to build a lime kiln. He got back about ten feet from the edge of the bluff and dug a hole about twelve feet in diameter, and then he went to the base of the bluff and dug a tunnel to connect with the hole. He built a fire box there out of railroad rails and some other old iron.

Then he filled that hole above the firebox with rock. We went down to the creek and we hauled round rocks and dumped them in that hole for a week. We filled up that hole with rocks and then we hauled up a lot of wood and started a big fire in the firebox under the rock. We didn't have mesquite, so we hauled cedar and oak wood. I guess we hauled up ten wagonloads of wood.

Papa started that fire, and for the first two hours, it looked like it wasn't going to burn, but finally it got enough heat in those rocks to cause a draft and, boy, it really started to burn. We had to have two men stoking that fire all the time. About four the next morning, Papa woke us up and told us to start hauling more wood. We kept that fire going until the rocks were red hot, and we couldn't see a spot on them.

After it all cooled, we pulled the firebox out of the hole so we could get the lime out, and then we hauled it to the house. You could take a twenty-pound rock and after it burned it wouldn't weigh ten pounds. We slaked the lime by piling the rocks up and wet them with water. The cooked rocks stayed together, but they were chalky, and when we sprinkled water on them they would disintegrate and turn to lime. They would get hot when you put water on them. You could drop a three- or four-pound rock in a five-gallon bucket, and you had to jump back because it would start bubbling and almost shoot the water out.

We mixed sand and water with the lime, and all of the rocks in that house were laid using lime.[5]

What They Ate

The settlers west of the Pecos not only had housing and water problems; they had food problems, too. In most parts of Texas, the pioneers had good soil and adequate water to grow food, but that was not the situation in the Langtry country. There was very little soil and very little rainfall. Ranch families that had enough water to grow a few vegetables usually had to haul in soil from the stockpens or from wide draws, where a little dirt had washed in.

Native plants were available for food, but most of them were seasonal. Several kinds of cacti had edible fruit in the spring and early summer. Young prickly-pear leaves were gathered in the spring and cooked in several different ways. In the summer, the prickly-pear apples could be eaten, although they were not as tasty as the more popular fruit of the pitaya cactus. Sometimes the folks living along the river could beat the birds to wild grapes.

Deer, javelina pigs, cottontail rabbits, dove, quail, and abundant catfish—in both the Pecos and the Rio Grande—were natural sources of meat. Varmints were commonly trapped in the winter for their hides, but—as Beula Burdwell Farley told me—sometimes raccoons were eaten. Mrs. Farley recalled:

> Pat and Sally Netherland lived up the river from us, and he was a fisherman and trapper. Mr. Netherland taught us how to trap coons. He said take the top off a sardine can that is bright. He showed us how to put it on the trigger of a trap and then set the trap in the water. The coons would pat at it with their foot and it would catch them every time.
>
> The Netherlands had the biggest old fish traps, and they would come down into our fishing place. We didn't like that but Pa had to get along with them. One time I was down there, and they pulled one out and there was water moccasins, and I don't know how many kinds of fish, turtles, frogs, and everything. We used to catch worlds of fish. Whenever we wanted a mess of fish we throwed a hook in and got it. It didn't make any difference whether we used mesquite beans for bait or what.[6]

Just about everybody ranching west of the Pecos had goats, and fried goat meat was an everyday staple food. Every household had chickens and eggs to eat, but only occasionally were steers killed. If an animal was killed in hot weather, often the meat was shared with neighbors, there being little ice to keep it from spoiling. Folks along the railroad could conveniently ship ice in, but for ranchers ice meant a trip to town, in addition to the expense, and most of them did without.

Most families had a few hogs. Horace Shackelford told me about hog-killing time:

> When we would see the first blue norther coming, we would start sharpening knives, building fires, and heating water. We would kill a hog and drag it up close to the big, iron pots full of hot

water and place it on some boards. We would then cover it with gunnysacks and pour scalding water on them and steam the hog until we could easily pull out the hair. Then we would scrape all of the hair off the carcass until it was clean and as white as it could be.

Then we would use a block and tackle and hang the hog to butcher it. After removing the insides, we cut it up. We didn't have meat saws, so we used an axe or hatchet to cut down the backbone and split the carcass in half. Then we quartered it.

We then would salt most of the meat by rubbing salt all over it and hang it where it was cool. We then put the meat in the smoke-house and smoked it for a few days.

A lot of the hog was made up into sausage. We would cook the sausage and put it in a five-gallon can and pour grease over it that we had melted from the fat. The grease would seal the meat and it would keep in the can for a long time.

We saved the ears, the snout, the tongue, and places like that to make souse. We would cut up all those parts and cook them in a pot with some seasoning, and it would form a kind of jelly when it cooled. We would eat souse cold, and it was good. I liked to cut a slab of it and put it in a biscuit and eat it. A lot of people had rather have the souse than anything.

We would cut all the fat from the belly parts and other parts of the hog to render for lard. We had to heat the fat slowly in the big, iron kettles so we could melt it without burning it. Then, sometime later, we would use it to make soap.

We would heat the fat and then put lye with it. We cooked it and stirred it until it got the right texture, and then we would let it cool overnight. The next day, we would slice up the soap into chunks. The homemade lye soap was used to wash clothes or whatever we needed it for. It was especially good to wash your hair with. It would keep forever.[7]

Even after the railroad penetrated Roy Bean's country, it was still a long way between grocery stores, and what the stores stocked was very limited. There were no facilities for keeping food in cold storage. Only the basic staples of beans, flour, lard, coffee, sugar, dried fruit, and canned goods were available. Wagon trips to the store were few and far between, so the staple goods were purchased in large quantities.

Rosa Babb Stapp had memories about food from her childhood in the early years of the century:

> We didn't eat as much in them days as we do now. We mainly had butter beans and black-eyed peas. Of course, there wasn't any such thing as pintos in them days. We had red beans that were a lot better than pintos. Mother and Daddy drank coffee and Mother parched the coffee. It was Peaberry coffee. We had a big old bread pan, and Mother would stand there and stir the coffee in the pan and parch it on the big wood stove.
>
> Of course, we didn't have ice, but we had lots of meat. We raised a few hogs for meat and killed them and salted them down. We dried our beef and cut it in strips and hung it on a wire to dry. If the flies were bad, we rolled it in cornmeal before we hung it up, 'cause then they wouldn't bother it.
>
> People just didn't eat as much in them days as they do now. We usually just had biscuits and gravy for breakfast, and we usually had molasses on hand if anybody wanted something sweet. Sometimes we would buy dried apples and dried peaches, and then my mother would make cobblers. Of course, we didn't have any preserves because we didn't have any jars to put them in. We didn't have any jars at all in them days. We didn't know what a jar was.
>
> Usually, during Christmastime, my mother would buy a wooden bucket of candy and that was about the only time we ever had candy.[8]

Lillie Burdwell Shelton, the youngest member of the Joe Burdwell family, lived on the Rio Grande about three miles upstream from Langtry. She told me what it was like going to school in Langtry and taking her lunch with her:

> The Cottolene lard bucket was the best thing to carry lunch in. Our mother did not know that she should have put little holes in the top of the bucket so that the lunch could get air, so our bread would always be wet from sweating in the bucket.

We brought our lunch in little lard buckets. They didn't have lunch meat in those days, so we would have fried goat meat or fried beef and sometimes Mama would give us a dime and we could go to Mr. Dodd's store to buy something else. Sometimes it was Dime Brand condensed milk—oh, that was good! But it cost a dime. Some days we would buy a nickel box of crackers and a nickel's worth of cheese.

To get to school, we had to walk down the river about two miles and then up Pump Canyon and climb out the steps. There were a hundred and ninety-six of them. Then we would walk down the railroad to Langtry.

When I started to school at Langtry, I just went to school one-half a day. I would walk in with the other kids in the morning and mother came in about noon when she brought her butter and milk to town to sell. She would ride into Langtry on a big white horse on a sidesaddle.

They always had a big Christmas tree in Langtry, and Mother and all of us kids would walk into town for the Christmas tree and then walk back home at night. There were lots of us in the family and we were poor. We were so rich in love and other things that we didn't know we were so poor. We didn't get anything, hardly, for Christmas. I remember one Christmas how happy I was when I got a little doll with a china head. That was all I got for Christmas, be-sides candy and an orange and an apple.

After the tree, we walked home, and it was bitterly cold. We walked down the railroad track west of Langtry and then went down the steps into Pump Canyon, crossed the canyon, and walked the river a couple of miles home. Before we got to Pump Canyon we stopped and built a fire and ate some candy and our apples; we really enjoyed having fruit and candy. It might sound pitiful today, but it was not to us—why we were so happy to have those things.[9]

People living in the towns along the railroad enjoyed a greater variety of foods than did the families living on ranches. Fresh food could be shipped by rail from Del Rio and San Antonio. Cross Dodd, who grew up in Langtry, recalled even having soft drinks:

The first soft drinks I can remember were made by my mother. She sent off and got the stuff to make soda water with. It was a kind of soft drink, and the only kind of soda water I knew about. She put it in a bottle with a rubber stopper, and when you wanted to drink it you pushed the stopper down. I don't know how Mother made soda water, but she would wash and scald the bottles and put this homemade drink in them. I don't think they had any soft drinks at Roy Bean's saloon.[10]

Ranchers did not get to town often, and it was always a thrill for the children when they had the opportunity to go to town for supplies. Women were glad to get to go to town to visit, but the men did almost all of the purchasing of supplies. Alfred Shelton gave me an example of the kind of problem that could arise:

When I first came here, there were two old boys living at the mouth of Reagan Canyon by the name of Lemmons—Henry and Bob Lemmons. One time, Henry came to town and got a bunch of groceries, and going back he was over there the other side of San Francisco Canyon, and he broke a wagon wheel, right in a narrow place. He couldn't move the wagon, and nobody could very well get by. He was not expecting any other wagons to be coming along there anyway, so he got on his horse and went on home to get another wagon, and come back the next day to get it.

There was a kind of tough fellow living over there on San Francisco, and he came along and turned Henry's wagon over so he could get by. When Henry got back to the wagon and saw what had happened, he went over to San Francisco Canyon and got that fellow and made him go back up there and straighten up the wagon and load up all his stuff.[11]

My father remembered the kinds of food he ate as a young man working on ranches in the Langtry area about 1915:

The basic staples of food that people west of the Pecos used were bread, potatoes, rice, coffee, chili, flour, beans, lard, and sugar.

Once in a while, they had canned tomatoes or canned corn. The people ate lots of meat—mainly goat meat.

A lot of the meat was dried. It could be used in hash, stewed, or boiled. Beef was dried in thick strips that would not get as dry and hard as most dried goat meat. Beef was cut in strips about an inch thick and eight or ten inches long. Then it would be salted and hung out to dry. If flies were bad, it would be rolled in corn meal to keep the flies off. After it was dried, it would usually be put in cloth sacks and hung up to be used as needed. Of course, after the meat was once dried, it would keep for a long time, but would usually be used up in a month or two.

If a cowhand was camped out, then he would throw the strips of dried meat on the coals of the camp fire and warm it up before eating it. Dried meat was almost always carried in saddlebags so that the cowboy could have something to eat when he got hungry. The dried meat gave him something to chew on until his jaws got too tired to fight it any longer.

The only kind of meat that was generally bought was salt pork. Hogs were a rarity, and salted pork would keep several months, so it was popular to have it on hand. Beans were the most common food and were expected almost every meal. Salt pork was used to season beans, rice, stew, and other camp dishes. The salt pork was also sliced, boiled, and then fried as bacon.

When I was working in Mexico, I generally carried some dried meat or a piece of bread and a piece of bacon in my saddlebag. When I got hungry, I'd kill a rabbit and dress it and then cut strips of bacon and wrap around the rabbit and stick them on with thorns. Then I would cook it over coals on a stick. The bacon grease sure gave the rabbit a good flavor.

Sometimes when we were in camp, we would eat armadillos, coons, hawks, and wood rats. Wood rats were good. When we lived in Pumpville, the section hands would go out rat hunting on Sundays. They would kill the rats where they nested in prickly-pear bunches and take them home to eat. I think they usually made chili out of them.

I went by a Mexican sheepherders camp one day and there was a skillet on the coals of his campfire. It had some kind of white meat in it. I thought it was quail, so I ate some. I rode on out, and after a while, I ran into the herder and told him I had eaten some of the meat he had in his skillet. I told him it sure was good and then asked him if it was quail. He laughed and said it was rattlesnake.

One time when I killed a bear in Mexico, I took a couple of big chunks of it into camp and ate it and it sure was good. I wished I had kept more of it, because it was just like pork.[12]

These early settlers west of the Pecos lived a simple, hardworking life. Their life was primitive, compared with the living standards to the east, but they had their freedom—and dreams of accumulating stock, to which we turn in the next chapter.

CHAPTER 6

---•••---

RANCHING

As more settlers began to enter Roy Bean's country, they started drilling wells and putting up windmills. Soon they had to start building fences. Livestock had ranged freely between the two big rivers and drifted wherever they could find food and water. Each spring, the ranchers got together for big cattle drives, generally beginning at the mouth of the Pecos and working westward. The cowboys gathered wild cattle out of the river vegas [*vega* is Spanish for *bottomland*], chased them out of the deep canyons, and ran them off the highest hills—always heading them westward. As the herd of strays moved through the country, each rancher cut out his stock, and by early summer all the ranchers again had their stock in the general vicinity of their ranch headquarters.

After sheep came into the region, huge flocks were moved each spring to the trans-Pecos's few shearing facilities. Smaller ranchers joined together in the shearing operation, and sheep were brought ten or fifteen miles to the central shearing pens. Ranchers with large spreads of land and thousands of sheep had their own facilities.

Dominick Hart, who we met in the preceding chapter and who had as many as ninety-five thousand sheep ranging on 250 sections of land, did his shearing at a shearing headquarters located on Lozier Canyon. For months before shearing time, a wood-gathering crew worked long days cutting wood and hauling it in wagons to the shearing pens, where it would be used to fire the boilers that furnished power for the clippers. When the shearing started, the woodpile would often be 15 feet high and 150 feet long. Rib wood or ironwood was generally used because it was easy to find and was brittle and easy to break. Along with mesquite, it provided a hot, long-burning fire for the boilers.

The steam engine that provided the power for shearing was mounted on a concrete block and had a power shaft about a hundred feet long. Pulleys on the shaft provided power to seventy drops, or shearing stations, allowing seventy men to be shearing at one time when the engine was at full capacity.

Even with sixty or seventy men working at the shearing pens, it would usually take over a month to shear the sheep on the Hart ranch.

Sheep scab, a skin disease caused by a parasite, was constantly a problem to the sheep ranchers, and each time the sheep were sheared they were also dipped. At the Lozier shearing pens, a long dipping vat was used for this purpose. Water for the vat was heated in a tin tank before it was placed in the vat. A mixture of lime and sulfur was put in the water to kill the scab, and after each sheep was sheared it was run through the vat.

The first fence in the lower trans-Pecos was what ranchers called a drift fence, which ran from bluff to bluff down Lozier Canyon. It was a three-strand barbed-wire fence that started at the railroad below the Lozier section house and followed Lozier Canyon. Bluffs along the canyon served as natural barriers to livestock much of the way; where there were no bluffs, the barbed wire was strung. This fence merely served to keep livestock from drifting out of that part of the country. But landowners soon began fencing their property, and some of the watering places that had been frequented by drifting stock were no longer accessible. As fencing became popular, it became necessary to drill wells.

The first wells west of the Pecos were drilled by the railroad in search of water to fill the boilers of steam locomotives. One of the first windmills to turn was at Lozier Canyon. A giant Eclipse mill with a twenty-five-foot wooden wheel was erected over a well drilled by the G. H. & S. A. Other early wells with windmills in the region prior to 1910 were at White Hat, Watkins, Seven Mile, and Windmill Tanks. All of these windmills were either Eclipse or Standard and had huge, wooden wheels. Most of the successful wells were drilled to depths between four hundred and a thousand feet. The early mills did not have gears, so the deep wells were pumped with mills with huge wheels.

In the early days of ranching, wells were generally drilled on low-lying land, so they would not have to go so deep to reach water. In later years, they were drilled on higher hills so that water could gravity-flow to troughs considerable distances from the wells.

Land, Lots of Land

It took lots of land to make ranching west of the Pecos profitable. The men working with livestock were often far from their ranch headquarters and spent much time camped out on the range. All members of a family shared in the ranch work and there was always plenty to do on a ranch. Myrtle Babb Cash was the youngest daughter of Bill Ike and Alice Babb. The Babbs owned one of the larger ranches in the Langtry area, and Myrtle grew up working on the ranch. She herded goats, broke horses, repaired fences, roped and doctored sick stock, and did any other work that needed to be done. After she married Roy Cash, she and her husband acquired part of the Babb ranch and operated it until their deaths many years later.

She spoke with me about what life on a ranch was like for a girl shortly after 1900:

When I was a kid, everyone in our family had to work. We all had our job, and Walter, Dillard, and I were the goatherders. We would go out every morning and herd the goats, and stay with them out in the hills all day, and then bring them back in the late afternoon, and pen them for the night. Sometimes we went horse-back and other times we went on foot.

I was about eight or nine years old then, and it was real lone-some staying out with a herd of goats all day, but we each got to know the goats so well that they were our friends. In fact, there was an old nannie in my herd that I had trained to get part of my dinner from. I generally had some sort of a lunch that I carried with me, and if I wanted milk to go with my lunch, I would bleat like a kid goat and that old nanny would stop, and come over to me and I would suck her. She had a little kid that needed that milk, but any-way, I got it. I generally didn't carry any water, but just drank out of potholes or cow tracks and many, many times when I got thirsty, I would call that old nanny and suck her—she had the prettiest long white teats.

Sometimes we would herd the goats back up in the high hills, and we would each leave our herd on different sides of the hills, and then we would get together to play. Walter had two dogs, Old Whitey and Yeller Boy, and I had one, Old Fanny, and we would leave the dogs to watch the goats. Then we would find a nest of wood rats, or pack rats, and we would set their nest afire and run them out and catch them. We would play like the rats were our horses, and we would neck them together and make teams out of them. The rats were hard to catch and they would bite like every-thing.

Sometimes we would use the dogs to catch them and as soon as the dogs grabbed them, the rats would sull [play dead], and we could get them before they were hurt. Sometimes we would have a whole string of rats tied together, and we would have more fun with these rats. We would get to playing with those rats, and before we would know it, it would be late and we would have to ride like drunk Indians to get the goats together again.

I had some dolls I made out of rags, and I kept them hidden in the pasture in a bucket that had a lid on it, and as I went out in the mornings, I would pick up my dolls and play with them most of the day, and put them back in the afternoon.[1]

Sheep and goats were kept in herds until about 1927. Most of the ranchers employed herders from Mexico, and these men lived with their flocks. On the larger ranches, a *vaciero* (head man for several flocks) was responsible for three or four flocks of goats and their *pastores* (herders). The herders drifted across the range most of the year, but in the spring they established kidding camps and herded the goats near the camps until all of the kid goats were old enough to graze with the nannies.

A typical kidding camp consisted of about a hundred small, A-shaped shelters built by leaning two flat rocks against each other. A third rock, across one end, completed a three-sided shelter. As kid goats were born, the herder staked them in front of a rock hut. A stake was driven into the ground at the open end of the hut and a wire swivel was tied to the stake. The herder made the swivels by bending the pointed end of a two-inch nail to form a circle about one-half of an inch across. A piece of wire about six inches long was formed into a triangle shape and both ends were looped around the head end of the first nail to complete the swivel. A heavy string or small rope was tied to the circular end of the nail with the other end tied to the stake. Another string, tied to the triangular end of the swivel, was attached to the kid's leg. If a nannie had twins, the swivel was made larger, of heavier wire, and swivels were attached to it for each kid.

Building fences in the rocky country cut by deep canyons has always been difficult in the lower trans-Pecos country. Each posthole was dug with a crowbar, and in that solid-rock country, it often took two or three hours to dig a single posthole. Ranchers had crowbars made of good steel, but they still had to be sharpened frequently. Many of the ranchers sharpened their own: they would heat the point of a bar to red hot in a forge and then hammer it on an anvil. It would then be filed to a good, sharp point and tempered. Some folks used oil in tempering, but most ranchers heated the point of the bar until it was red and then barely touched it in a bucket of water before holding it above the water and watching for a blue line to rise up the metal from the point. The bar was then quickly dropped into the water to cool. It was a true craft, and men were respected for their ability to put a good temper in a bar.

Ranchers in Roy Bean's country always wanted rain. However, a good rain usually meant that fences had to be fixed; the so-called water gaps would have washed away or been damaged. There was little grass in the rocky country, and when it rained hard much of the water swiftly flowed down the canyons and washed away the fences in the canyon bottoms. Ranchers soon learned that fences crossing draws and canyons should be tied loosely, so that when a flood occurred a loose end of fence would swing down the canyon—thus creating a water gap. The rancher then had merely to swing the fence back into position and tie it. Other types of water gaps were created by fences suspended from cables stretched across the canyon. The bottoms of such fences were held in place by occasional rocks. When the canyons flooded, the rocks, not the fences, washed away, and the fences swung freely in the current.

As some of the ranchers prospered, they occasionally leased land across the Rio Grande in Mexico. Some had stock grazing on hundreds of sections of land on both sides of the river. The livestock was often moved back and forth across the Rio Grande.

The main crossings on the Rio Grande above the mouth of the Pecos were:

Eagle Nest Crossing—located just downstream from the eagle nest on the bluff opposite the town of Langtry.

Rathbone Crossing—about three miles up river from Langtry and named for a man named Rathbone who built a house near the crossing.

Rattlesnake Crossing—seven miles up river from Langtry, just above the mouth of Rattlesnake Canyon.

Ramsey Crossing—located a short distance above the mouth of Ramsey Draw and named after a man who built a house near the point where the draw runs into the Rio Grande. One of the Ramsey children was buried at this site. Just above Ramsey Draw, on the opposite side of the river, was where Hiporte Garcia had his ranch house. During the Mexican Revolution, a raid was made on this ranch house. Three people were killed in the raid and their bodies were thrown into the well near the house.

Pool Crossing—a little-used crossing a short distance upstream from Ramsey Crossing.

Paso Fuentes Crossing—below Lozier Canyon; named after a Mexican rancher who had a small rock house on the Mexican side of the river at the site of this crossing. Many cattle were brought out of Mexico here during the Mexican Revolution and were run through a dipping vat adjacent to the rock house.

Lozier Crossing—located just below the mouth of Lozier Canyon.

Mesquite Crossing—several miles upstream from Lozier, where Parita Canyon runs into the Rio Grande from the Mexican side of the river.

Shafter Crossing—south of Dryden; named after Colonel William R. Shafter, who led a group of soldiers chasing Indians across the Rio Grande at this location.

These crossings on the Rio Grande were places where the river was shallow enough for cattle to be driven across and where there were trails coming to the water on both sides of the river. Sheep were occasionally taken across the river, but it was generally much more difficult to get them across the swift Rio Grande.

My dad, Guy Skiles, told of bringing six thousand sheep across the Rio Grande at Rathbone Crossing:

> Jim White had a big bunch of sheep over in Mexico and had a fellow named Tom Williamson taking care of them. I don't know whether Williamson got in trouble with the Mexican officials or not, but he could not go back to the ranch, so Jim White sold the sheep to J. R. Hamilton. I was working for old man Hamilton at the time, and he wanted me to go over and bring the sheep out of Mexico for him.
>
> I crossed the river at Villa Acuña on the sixth day of May and rode about twenty miles out to San Gregorio, which is on the Las Vacas River. Fred Bedham was at San Gregorio, and he helped me pen the sheep there. We paint-branded all the ewes and lambs and put a different number on the sheep in each herd, so that if they ran

together I could separate them and get the right ewes and lambs together.

A hailstorm hit us just out of San Gregorio and killed about fifty or sixty head of the sheep, but we got on up to Rathbone Crossing on the eighteenth of May. Ed Foster met me at the crossing with two wagons loaded with cable and lumber, and we proceeded to build a bridge across the river to cross the ewes and lambs on.

We put two wagons out in the middle of the river and then stretched two cables across the river above the wagons. We dug deep holes in the gravel on each side of the river and put big logs in the holes to anchor the cables to. We tied a piece of three-inch pipe to the cables and wrapped the cables around it about three times, using Stilson wrenches to turn the pipe with to get the cables tight. When we got the cables as tight as we could, we then clamped them in position.

The cables swung about two feet above the river. We then proceeded to build the bridge about two hundred feet long and two feet wide. The framework for the bridge was made of two-by-four boards fastened to the cable, and then one-by-four boards were nailed to the frame to make the sides and bottom. The wagons were placed under the bridge to give it more support and kept it from swaying back and forth.

We did not have any trouble getting the sheep to cross on the bridge and got all six thousand head of them crossed in one day. We drove them on up to Antonio Creek, near Pumpville. The law required that anything brought out of Mexico had to be dipped twice, so we sheared and dipped them at the pens on Antonio Creek. The night we finished shearing them it came a big rain and got pretty cold. I went out the next morning and found dead sheep all over the country. Some of them froze down and died just laying on their hunkers—they just looked like they were laying there asleep and weren't even turned over on their side. They had just been sheared and dipped, and they were hungry and just didn't have enough resistance to survive that cold night. We lost about five hundred head of sheep that night.[2]

My father, who worked on ranches along the Rio Grande for several years, also related experiences about working on the Mexican side of the river:

In 1924, I was working for Jim White when he leased the hundred-thousand-acre Consuelo Ranch in Mexico, across from Dryden. He paid a hundred dollars a month for it. During the Mexican Revolution, all of the ranchers in northern Mexico that were close to the Rio Grande had brought their cattle to the United States and sold them. There hadn't been any stock on the Consuelo Ranch for years, and there was lots of grass, so Jim White leased it and sent me over there to run it from 1924 until 1926.

We took a thousand head of dry cows to Mesquite Crossing in September of 1924, but when we got there the river was up and too swift to cross, so we held the cattle at the mouth of Bear Canyon. There was nothing we could do but wait until the river went down, and the area between Bear Canyon and the river was an ideal place to hold a herd of cattle. There were bluffs on two sides of the herd and we only had to watch the other two sides.

In a few days, the river went down enough for us to cross them. There was an island in the river, so we put them on the island and night-herded them all night. About daylight the next morning, an old bull that had been staying there on the river just swum across the river to the Mexican side and the whole herd followed him. It wasn't but just a few minutes until all the cattle were over there.

We moved them up the river a'ways and then started toward the headquarters of the Consuelo Ranch. That night we camped at a water hole. Jim and George Burdwell, Henry Hillburn, the Farley boy, Alfred White, a fellow named Boatright and I were all camped there together.

The next morning before daylight, George Burdwell and I were just starting to get up when Alfred White hollered for us to come over and help him. He said a snake had bit him.

Well, I thought maybe a stinging scorpion had bit him, and I said, "Aw, you haven't got snake bit, you haven't even got out of your bedroll yet."

Alfred hollered back and said, "Hell, he's in bed with me."

George and Jim Burdwell doctoring a horse in 1923.

So George jumped up and put on his boots and ran over there. He struck a match and threw Alfred's cover back, and sure enough, there was a damn copperhead in there. Alfred must have rolled it up in his bedroll the morning before when we were camped by the river.

Everybody got up and I went over there to try to help. Somebody built up a fire and a couple of men went out to get the saddle horses up, and somebody got Alfred a quart of tequila from a bootlegger that had camped there with us. Alfred sat up in his bedroll and started drinking it.

I had my bag with me with all my clothes in it, and I had a straight razor in my bag. I got my razor and cut a pretty big gash on the instep of his foot where the snake had bit him. Alfred had a can of permanganated potash that he carried for snakebite medicine, so he told me to put it in a cup and mix some water with it and put it on the bite. The permanganated potash was little black grains and looked kinda like gunpowder. I mixed up a paste of it and asked Alfred how much of it to put on the snakebite and he said, " Hell, put it all on there."

Well, I put it on the cut place and then took a leather saddle string and tied it around his leg for a tourniquet, a little above his instep. By that time, Alfred was getting pretty scared and wanted me to write out his will, so I sat down there and wrote down on a tablet what he told me to write. He was drinking tequila all that time. He drank about a whole bottle while he was sitting there.

In a little while, a Mexican came into camp with the saddle horses, and George Burdwell sent him to Dryden to get someone there to phone Del Rio for a doctor. Jim Burdwell went to the Consuelo Ranch house to get Alfred's suitcase and clothes, and George and the rest of us were going to take him towards the river. Henry Hillburn struck a lope to go across the river to Max Lucky's camp. That was the nearest ranch house on the American side, and he was going to borrow Lucky's car so we could get Alfred to Dryden quicker.

We put Alfred on a gentle horse of George Burdwell's, and George and I started out to the river with him. We got about a mile from camp and by that time Alfred was getting so drunk he couldn't hardly ride. He was sitting there with his leg over the horn of the saddle and he was happy. He had forgot about the damn snakebite. I was riding a little ways behind Alfred, and I saw he was getting pretty wobbly, so I told Jim, "Catch Alfred's horse and lead him, 'cause he is going to fall off that horse in a minute."

When I said that, Alfred said, "Fall off hell, I'm all right."

He was riding by a lechuguilla stalk, and he reached out and broke the stalk off and jobbed that old horse in the neck with it. The old horse gave a big jump and Alfred fell off. Somehow, he fell under the horse's belly and the horse stepped on his head. It knocked Alfred out and he was just laying there with blood running out of his ears. It scared hell out of us, and George said, "Hell, I believe that horse killed him."

I got off my horse and looked at Alfred a little closer and told George, "Aw, he's all right. You go back to camp and get the Mexicans with the herd to come help us."

There was a pothole of water there close, and I got George to help me drag Alfred over to the pothole and help me prop him against a dagger [a yucca-type plant]. By that time the sun was coming up. George lit out back to camp to get Boatright and the Mexicans. I got a hat full of water and poured it on Alfred and got him to come to a little bit. George and the other fellows got back pretty quick so we put him [Alfred] on a horse and I got on behind him to hold him in the saddle, and we started to the river.

Alfred was crazy drunk by then and was fighting me all the time. He had drunk better than a quart of tequila. I had both arms around him and was holding on to the high brass horn of the saddle and holding him on the horse. He kept beatin' the saddle horn, trying to get me to turn loose, but he was just beatin' on that brass horn. I don't know how he managed to do it, but d'reckly he reached around and knocked my hat off and got a hand full of my hair. He leaned over and we both fell off the horse.

The other fellows helped me get Alfred back on the horse, and we finally got him to the bluff above the river. The trail leading off the bluff to the river was awfully rough, and I don't think any of us had ever been off the bluff there at that trail before. We stopped and left a Mexican to stay with Alfred while we went down to see how the trail went and to figure out the best way to get him down there. We finally picked out the best way to the river and decided we would put Alfred in a saddle blanket and carry him down to the water. We got back up to where we had left Alfred, and the old Mexican was way off over there on the side of the hill, and Alfred was sitting up and throwing rocks at him. He was crazier than hell.

We told Alfred we had to carry him down the bluff to the river, and he said, "All right," so we put him in a blanket and the four of us got hold of the blanket, one on each corner, and finally got him down to the edge of the water. The river was up three or four feet and was real swift, and we didn't know how we were going to get Alfred across the river. I was afraid that if we tried to swim the river horseback, that Alfred might fall off and drown, but somebody said, "Well hell, he might just as well to drown as stay over here and die," so I got on the horse with Alfred and held him on, and George led the horse. A man got on each side and one behind us, and we started out.

We didn't have to swim but the water got way up on the saddle. We got him across the river all right and up the bluff on the American side and then started looking for Henry Hillburn with the car. The old Mexican scouted around some and found Henry had gotten a car from Max Lucky, all right, but he had started to the river and gotten stuck in a canyon. We went out to help Henry and found that the Model T car wouldn't run. I got to fooling with it and took the magneto plug out and cleaned it off and got it started.

We drove on towards the river and got Alfred loaded into the car and started to Dryden with him. When we got about halfway to Dryden, we met John Gist and somebody else in an old Nash car. The Mexican had already gotten to Dryden and phoned a doctor at Del Rio. John Gist was at Pumpville and happened to be on the line and found out about Alfred getting bit, so he got in his car and came up there to meet us.

We put Alfred in John Gist's car and George and I was going to go on back to the river and on to our camp in Mexico. Alfred had sobered up enough to talk, and he said, "Hell no. Come on and go with me. You have brought me this far and have to take me on."

We got in Gist's car then and went on to Dryden and stopped and phoned to see if the doctor was on the way. We found out that he had left Del Rio a long time before. While we were in Dryden, we got some coal oil and salt and put on Alfred's foot, and a lot of people came out to the car. Alfred was in a hell of a shape but he was able to talk.

A couple of women came out there and one of them said, "That's the first time I ever saw anybody snakebit with blood running out of both ears and his nose."

Alfred said, "Aw, these fellows beat hell out of me."

One of the women looked sort of shocked and said, "Well what did you put on that snake bite?"

Alfred look up at her and said, "Everything from horse piss to tequila."

That shut the woman up and they went back in the store.

We came on down the dirt road toward Del Rio and met Jim White and Doctor York right in the middle of Lozier Canyon at about five that evening. Alfred had gotten bit at about five that morning, and we got him to the doctor at about five that evening.

The doctor looked at him, and the first thing he said was, "How long has that tourniquet been on there?"

I said, "Ever since he got snakebit this morning. I put it on there this morning before daylight, and it has been on there ever since."

The doctor said, "Well, it wasn't tight enough to cut all the blood off, or he would have lost his foot."

I guess the leather string had gotten loosened by Alfred stomping around and raising hell all day.

Doctor York examined Alfred and finally looked up at us and said, "If what ya'll have done to him hasn't killed him already, then he is bound to get over the snake bite."

They took Alfred on to town and George and I went on back to Mexico. That permanganated potash ate a big hole out of the top of Alfred's foot just like acid had been poured on it, and it took a long time to heal. When the horse stepped on his head and shoulder it had broken his collar bone, but in about three months he was all right.[3]

Sheep and cattle were frequently crossed back and forth along the Rio Grande, but those coming into the United States were supposed to be cleared by U. S. Customs inspectors. Many of the ranchers along the border did not want to go to the trouble of notifying the customs men and then waiting for them to arrive to observe the crossing of the stock, nor were they anxious to pay the duty fees on stock brought out of Mexico; the customs service and the Texas Rangers therefore kept a close watch on activities along the river. Dad had a good story about this:

I was living in Mexico, across from Sanderson, and John Gist brought me some grub and left it at Max Lucky's camp, close to Shafter Crossing. Max was smuggling and had a bunch of goats, mares, and horses that he had brought out of Mexico. The rangers were up there chasing him around and rounding up all his stock, but I did not know anything about it. I knew my grub was supposed to be at Lucky's camp on a certain day, so I took a couple of Mexicans and a packhorse and crossed the river and went over to get it. When I got to Lucky's camp, Charley Carter was there and he told me that Texas Ranger Archie Miller and another ranger had been there that day but had gone to Dryden to meet the train because the chief customs officer from El Paso, with another fellow, was coming in to round up all of Max Lucky's stuff and seize it.

Charley told me that I had better get the Mexicans back across the river with the horses, so I loaded them up with grub and told them to go on. They all had guns on. The men pulled out for the river, and I stayed there to write some letters and send them in.

After a while Arch Miller and the customs men came in, and they asked Charley Carter who I was.

Charley said, "Oh, he works for the Block-Y ranch."

The officers were getting ready to ride towards the river, so while they were getting up their horses I decided it was time for me to leave. The river had been up and backed up in the canyon that Max Lucky's ranch was on and had left a lot of mud near the mouth of the canyon. The main trail went off the west side of the canyon, and you had to cross the canyon and go down below it to cross the river into Mexico. I knew that I couldn't get through the mud at the mouth of the canyon, so I crossed way up the canyon and worked my way along the east side of it.

Well, the rangers had seen me heading toward the river and wondered what the hell I was going that way for, so they took after me. I had about a mile head start on them and saw them coming, so I ducked off into the canyon and headed across the river. Just as I was crossing the river, the lawmen hollered at me to come back. When I wouldn't do it, Arch Miller came running his horse down the trail trying to head me off.

I had some steel traps where the trail went off on the west side of the canyon and that morning I had waded across the mud to get them. The ranger saw my tracks in the mud, and in his hurry he thought it was horse tracks. He ran his horse off in there, and it bogged up just as I was getting away on the Mexican side of the river.

A few days later, I was riding along on the Mexican side of the river and saw Max Lucky and hollered at him. I started to go across the river and he said, "Don't you come over here. Those damn rangers are looking for you. It took them until way after night to get that horse out of the bog hole, and they are damn sure waiting to get you."[4]

Dad managed the large ranch in Mexico for about two years. It was an outdoor life of working with livestock, riding over the range almost every day, observing nature, and sometimes being lonesome. He told about life on the range:

We never did have a tent and in the wintertime when it got real cold we either got in a cave or just camped out in the cold. We had a big tarp that we rolled the bedroll in and that was all the protection we had. If it rained, we got wet. Of course, we always kept a slicker tied on the back of the saddle. If it rained at night, then we just rolled up the bedroll to keep it dry and sat up on the bedroll with a slicker on all night. Of course, it didn't rain much.

When we were carrying our camp outfit, we usually carried it in two wooden gasoline boxes. In the early days of automobiles, gasoline came in five-gallon cans with two cans being packed in a hardwood case. These wooden boxes were real good for pack boxes. We would drill a hole in them on the side and pretty close to the top and then run a rope through the holes. After tying a knot in the rope so it would not slip through the holes, we would leave a loop in the rope that could be looped over the packsaddle on each side. The boxes would be full of grub and a cooking outfit, and we would tie our bedding on top of that and tie it down with a diamond hitch. Sometimes, when two of us were camping together, we would have two packhorses, one for grub and one for bedding.

When we were camped on the ranch in Mexico, we would get most of our grub out of Villa Acuña. When the freight wagon would come to the ranch with salt and other ranch supplies, they would bring us grub. We would generally get one hundred pounds of cornmeal, a hundred-pound sack of green coffee, a five-gallon

Guy Skiles and Ross Anderson with a mountain lion they killed in Mexico. Lions frequently killed livestock and were usually hunted with dogs. Anderson, right, was one of the few African-American cowboys in the Langtry area.

can or two of cottonseed oil to cook with, piloncillo (cone-shaped cubes of brown sugar) for sugar, and flour, and canned goods.

Besides using the cottonseed oil to cook with, we would also use it in a light. I would pour some oil in a can and twist a rag and put in it for a wick.

Sometimes we would go into Dryden to get grub, and we would take it back to camp on a packhorse. One time, a Negro named Ross Anderson and I were taking grub back to camp and we had two sacks of flour tied on a packhorse. One of the sacks got snagged on a limb, and the horse got scared when he saw the flour pouring out. He took off a'running and pitching and scattered flour until every bit of it was poured out.

With just two of us camping together, bathing and keeping our clothes clean wasn't much of a problem. We never would see anybody, so we didn't wash our clothes but about once a month. I only carried one change of clothes. For several months, a Mexican and I were camped at an old house in Mexico, and we got all of our

The author's father, Guy Skiles, with the rifle, pistol, and cartridge belt he wore while a ranch foreman in Mexico shortly after the Mexican Revolution.

water out of a water hole in the canyon in front of the house. We kept a five-gallon can down there and about once a month, on a warm day, we would go down there and build up a fire and go in the water hole and take a bath and change clothes. We would put the ones we pulled off in the five-gallon can with a bar of soap and boil them. We would punch them around with a stick, and after they had boiled about thirty minutes, we would rinse them and hang the clothes on a bush to dry. Then we would have a change of clean clothes to put on the next time we took a bath. A bath once a month was often enough—but of course sometimes we would be down on the river in the summertime and would go in swimming once in a while. Hell, there wasn't any reason to take a bath.

It was completely unheard of to carry a toothbrush. I kept one at the ranch headquarters, but never did brush my teeth unless I was going somewhere. When me and my partner got back to the ranch headquarters, we would occasionally cut each other's hair with a pair of scissors. Lots of times we would go six months without a haircut.[5]

The sheep ranchers, when they were not doctoring the sheep for screwworms, were trapping and hunting predators. Coyotes, bobcats, and mountain lions frequently killed stock, and they were hunted and trapped year-round. Big herds of wild donkeys ranging west of Langtry were another threat. Dad had memories of the wild donkeys and horses:

There was a bunch of about eighty-five wild donkeys that stayed near the mouth of Rattlesnake Canyon and between there and Langtry. We had lots of trouble with them killing sheep. The herders would take a flock of sheep into the watering places, and a bunch of those wild burros would come in there and paw and kill the lambs. The stud jacks would get after a sheep and run and paw after it and kick it until they killed it.

I was working for Hal Hamilton, and one spring the donkeys got to killing a whole lot of sheep. Something had to be done, so Hal bought a bunch of ammunition and sent me and Robert and Henry Elledge to kill as many donkeys as we could. We rode down to the mouth of Rattlesnake and found about fifteen donkeys in one bunch, between the canyon and the river. We had them hemmed in, and we got on a point of the bluff and went to shooting at them. I guess we shot seventy-five times, and we killed the whole dang bunch. It sounded like a war with Mexico was going on down there.

The author's father, Guy Skiles, on his horse Sundown. He has roped a calf, to be branded by Pleas Wallace and two other ranch hands on the Rattlesnake Ranch west of Langtry.

All together, we killed about eighty-five head of wild donkeys in that general area. They were the hardest animals to kill I ever shot at, and I have killed lots of bear, panther, and other wild animals. We hated to kill all those donkeys, but they were so mean we had to get rid of them.

By 1914, all of the wild horses had been caught in that country except four that stayed around Myers Springs. Martin and Willie Hart wanted to catch them, so we took about thirty-five or forty head of saddle horses out there and thought maybe we could get the wild horses in with the herd and drive them all into a pen. We would drive the wild ones into the herd, and they would just run out the other side and keep going. We then decided that we would run the wild horses until we could rope them.

The next morning, we cut out the best horses we had and took five or six Mexican ranch hands to help us. I only weighed about a hundred pounds and was the lightest man in the bunch, so I was the one to run the horses down. We sent the Mexicans in different directions with good horses and spotted them on certain hills to wait there until I came by running the wild horses. We then located the wild horses and I took after them. I really billed to them [got a

J. R. Skiles, the author's grandfather, foreman of the O Ranch at Rattlesnake Crossing on the Rio Grande.

fast start] and ran them full speed for two or three miles and came to a point where a man was waiting with another horse. I jumped off my horse and put my saddle on a fresh horse and took after 'em again.

I changed horses four or five times that morning, and finally, I could run up alongside the wild horses and whip them with my quirt. They stayed together pretty well most of the time, but finally, two of them dropped out, and we were able to catch only two of the wild horses. The next day we went back and did the same thing and caught the other two wild horses. We took them to the ranch and put hackamores on them and tied them to railroad ties so they could drag them and learn how to rein. After a couple of days, we started gentling them.

When I was running the ranch in Mexico for Jim White, there were still wild horses there. I came into my camp on Swerco Draw one evening, and a strange Mexican was there, and he had a three-year-old mare with a hackamore on her and a burro.

As I rode up, this fellow was eating, and he came over where I was unsaddling my horse, and he asked me if I had any worm medicine. I told him there was a bottle over by the camp in a bush, so he went and got it and walked out there and sat down behind that mare and picked up her hind foot and poured worm medicine on a rope burn on her hind feet and she just stood there. You just didn't hardly ever see any horses that gentle in Mexico in those days, so I asked him where he got that mare. He said, "I caught her."

I asked him "Well, how did you catch her?"

He said, "I put her in a pen over at the Consuelo Ranch."

I said, "Well, how in the hell did you ever pen her?"

He said, "I had a burro."

Well, I couldn't figure how a man could catch a wild horse and pen her with a burro, so I said, "You mean you penned that wild mare on a burro?"

He said, "Yeah, I penned a bunch of them."

Well, I still couldn't figure that, so I says, "Well, how long did it take you?"

He said, "About a week."

He had followed that bunch of wild horses day and night on that burro for about a week. I later found out his name was Cisto Gaytan, and he said he finally got the wild horses to where he could handle them and finally got them in a pen. He then had picked out a mare, roped her, saddled her up, and started breaking her. He was a good horsebreaker and was real good with horses. After he had doctored the mare's foot, he turned the burro loose.

One of the ways of catching wild horses over there was by creasing them. They would shoot them in the top of the shoulders and hit that muscle in the neck, in front of the shoulders, and it would paralyze them for a few minutes—long enough to get to them and tie them up. They would kill about a dozen wild horses for every one they caught. I tried it once and shot the horse too low on the shoulder and killed it.

Most of the wild horses were not very good. They were inbred and were little Spanish ponies.[6]

One of the biggest problems for ranchers in Roy Bean's country has always been drought. Those whose livelihoods depend on the growing of grass, weeds, or shrubs expect about fourteen inches of rain a year, but sometimes there would be a few years with only a fraction of that amount. In the earlier days of ranching, drought meant that ranchers had to sell much of their livestock, ship the animals away to greener country, or wait for rain and risk stock dying. In later years, supplemental feed could be purchased, but there was always the threat that a rancher might have to buy feed for so long that he would go broke.

Alfred (Big Boy) Shelton told me about having too many horses during a drought:

> When I first went to that country, I had sixteen good mares and a stallion. It was big open country with lots of grass and my horses just accumulated.
>
> In about 1930, it got dry, and I couldn't keep that big bunch of horses any longer and they weren't worth anything. They were beginning to fence up that country, and I couldn't keep them. The soap factory would have given me about three dollars and fifty cents a head, but I wouldn't take that. I gathered up four hundred head and cut back a few and carried more than three hundred head down to the mouth of Reagan Canyon and threw them over into Mexico. They were good horses, too.
>
> It was a pretty sight, seeing them three hundred-odd horses going down Reagan Canyon. When they smelled water in the Rio Grande, they struck a trot and went to the river.
>
> Those horses all had my brand on them and for several years Mexicans from Múzquiz and Quatro Cienegas would come by my ranch and say, "I've seen horses with that half-circle-S brand down to Múzquiz."[7]

Ranching west of the Pecos: always a risky business, with lots of hard work and hardship—but those who grew up in the business usually could not be happy doing anything else.

CHAPTER 7

LANGTRY

Flat land is hard to find in the rough, dry country west of the Pecos. Water is even more scarce. Consequently, it is no wonder that a town grew up on the greasewood flat opposite the big eagle nest on the Rio Grande. Springs of cool, clear water flowed in deep canyons just east and west of Langtry, and the main street of the town ran to the edge of the cliff cut out of the rock by the waters of the Rio Grande.

High on a bluff on the Mexican side of the river, a huge eagle nest has served as a prominent landmark of the trans-Pecos country as long as the white man can remember. The nest consists of a pile of sticks skillfully placed by eagles under a protective overhang near the top of a two hundred-foot cliff. The size of the nest indicates that it was used for many, many seasons. Still in excellent condition in 1996, it has not been used by eagles since before the turn of the century.

Lieutenant Bullis and other Indian fighters often trailed Indians to the crossing on the Rio Grande a few hundred yards below the eagle nest, and these military men undoubtedly camped near the crossing. Cavalry units and other adventurers traveling through the area also rode down to the gravel bars on the Rio Grande near the eagle nest to water their horses.

Beginning about 1870, ranchers along the Rio Grande began experiencing problems with raiders from Mexico crossing the river to steal livestock and take it back to Mexico. In 1872, ranchers began filing claims against the Mexican government, seeking reimbursment for their losses.[1] These claims were registered with the U.S. government, and as a result, the U. S. Cavalry began patrolling the Mexican border. Outposts of Fort Clark, called camps, were established at Eagle Pass, San Felipe Springs, Eagle Nest, and other points along the river to facilitate the river patrol. There was little ranching activity west of the Pecos, but soldiers camped at Eagle Nest served as a deterrent to both Mexican raiders and Indians crossing the area.

The temporary camp called Eagle Nest was established at the top of the bluff on the west side of Eagle Nest Canyon, overlooking the spring. It consisted of small stacked-rock structures and tents. No white man lingered in the area long enough to establish residence until 1878, when, as noted earlier, Jesus Torres, son of Cesario, moved onto the land opposite the nest. But we must pick up the Torres family story from an earlier date.

Cesario Torres and his brothers, Bernardo and Juan, were prominent citizens of Fort Stockton. They owned a considerable amount of land in Pecos County, and Cesario served as a county commissioner in Pecos County for many years. The Torres brothers, along with Felís Garza, organized the Torres Irrigation and Manufacturing Company, and one of their projects was the construction of a dam and irrigation system on the Pecos river about eight miles south of the present town of McCamey. The project was completed in 1877, and as payment for their work, they received from the State of Texas thirty-seven land certificates of 640 acres each. This land was in the vicinity of Eagle Nest Crossing on the Rio Grande.[2]

Land scrip No. 24 was transferred to Bernardo Torres, representing the company, on October 16, 1877, but it was not until July 24, 1882, that Governor O. M. Roberts formally granted Torres title to the section of land where the town of Langtry would be located. Meantime, Bernardo Torres had died; his brother Cesario purchased the land on the Rio Grande from his widow.

In 1882, railroad construction was going full blast in the area, and the construction camp called Eagle Nest was located on Torres land. The *San Antonio Evening Light* of September 2, 1882, had the following description of the tent town, written by Fred Locker:

Eagle Nest is one of the most peculiar places in the state. It lies in a valley and yet is considerably above the Rio Grande. It is now quite a city of tents, upwards of 300 being scattered around; some of them being 50 by 100 ft. The only wood building being the store of Max Meyer, who has a good stock and does a good business.

There are, at the lowest estimates 20 saloons and gambling tents, two tents of ill fame, and a dance hall, which is on full run every Sunday and two or three times a week. Two soiled doves from San Antonio have alighted here in their flight, and have made things lively at the dance halls. The dancing here is a la vaudeville. The

The village that was later named Langtry was called Eagle Nest before the railroad was completed. The name was taken from the eagle's nest near the top of a clifff across the border in Mexico. Still intact today, the long abandoned nest has been an area landmark for more than a hundred years.

quadrilles consisting of two figures; Figure 1. Fours right and left, back to places, swing on corners, all promenade.

Figure 2. Promenade to the bar. Drinks 50¢.

The most curious thing, and still more amusing is the action of Roy Bean. Roy is Justice of the Peace and holds court in a tent 16 × 18. Not more than 30 yards from his court is the justice's saloon and gambling tent where drink is freely dispensed and a dozen monte tables are in full blast. And it is no uncommon thing for suckers to get full in the Justices saloon and sleep off the effects in his court, not as a prisoner, but as a guest.

Rails from the west reached Eagle Nest in October 1882, and the hills and bluffs around the tent village loudly echoed the jubilance. The rowdy construction men were always looking for an excuse to celebrate and the arrival of the rails provided a perfect opportunity.

Why Langtry?

The village of Eagle Nest would be known by that name for only a short time. The railroad gave a new name to their station near the big eagle nest: Langtry. Later, they would claim that it was named in honor of a construction engineer, George Langtry, who helped build the railroad. Judge Bean claimed he named the town after Lillie Langtry, the English actress.

When the rails reached Langtry, construction was immediately begun on facilities for the new station. Langtry was to be a stop where fuel and water would be provided for the steam locomotives, and there was also to be a depot, with houses for a stationmaster, telegraph operators, a section foreman, and section workers. The depot, 105 feet long and 20 feet 9 inches wide, would be the center of activity in the new railroad town.

The steam locomotives, fired with coal, required a large amount of water for the boilers—and, as previously noted, water was the main reason for the establishment of the Langtry station. It was abundant in a deep canyon three-fourths of a mile west of the depot. At Torres Spring, located in a narrow gorge with walls more than two hundred feet deep, water was clear, and to insure an adequate reserve, a rock dam, four feet thick at the top and about eight feet high, was built across the solid-rock bottom of the canyon. A steam engine was installed a short distance above the dam to pump the water to a steel tank at Langtry. The deep canyon became thus known as

The Langtry depot, built in 1882, was located between Judge Bean's saloon and the Southern Pacific tracks. The long building had a loading dock, warehouse, telegraph office, waiting room, and restaurant.

Torres Spring in Pump Canyon, dammed in 1882. A pump was installed to provide water for the railroad and the town of Langtry. A wooden staircase that accessed the canyon was burned in 1968 after the Southern Pacific abandoned the facility.

Carranzistas, followers of Venustiano Carranza, at a cave they used as local headquarters across the Rio Grande from Langtry during the Mexican Revolution. (Photo courtesy of Western History Collections, University of Oklahoma.)

Pump Canyon. Farther up the canyon, it was always called Osman Canyon. In later years, the steam engine was replaced by a two-cylinder Fairbanks Morse diesel. A water-treatment plant was installed in 1926.

Wooden stairs were constructed into the canyon so the pumper could get down to the pump house. The 196 steps became a landmark almost as prominent as the eagle nest on the Rio Grande. They were used until April 1968, when the railroad burned the rickety stairs after abandoning the Pump Canyon facility.

The G. H. & S. A. laid tracks through Torres's land, erected buildings, built a dam, and made other improvements, but it was not until May 19, 1886 that a written agreement was made between Cesario Torres and the railroad. Torres conveyed a 150-foot-wide right-of-way through his lands, and transferred the Torres Spring property to the company with the provision that Torres and his family would receive free water. The railroad was also given one-half interest in 320 acres of land comprising the Langtry townsite laid out by the G. H. & S. A. At the time of the agreement, Jesus Torres lived in Langtry and managed his father's interests. He operated a saloon/store and also had a goat dairy. For a time he was also postmaster.[3]

Local legend has it that the agreement between Torres and the railroad prohibited the railroad from selling any land to Roy Bean, but the actual agreement—on file with Val Verde County—contains no such statement.

About a year later, Cesario Torres turned over his one-half interest in the Langtry townsite to the Southern Development Company, a corporation organized under the laws of the State of California, that was affiliated with the Southern Pacific Railroad.

Even before the railroad was completed in 1883, most of the construction people had moved from Langtry. But the boisterous frontier village was already beginning to take on a look of permanency. A number of railroad personnel were stationed at the new town; and ranchers, merchants, and saloon keepers were building permanent residences there.

Because Langtry was a border town, the U.S. government had had soldiers stationed there intermittently for many years. Shortly after the railroad was finished, troops were again stationed at Camp Langtry. In addition to guarding the border, the camp furnished forage for army units that still moved across West Texas by horse and wagon.

Camp Langtry was usually garrisoned by twenty enlisted men and a lieutenant. The cavalrymen were sent out from Fort Clark, and the tour of

The first school building in Langtry. The addition on the left end of the building was done with money donated by actress Lillie Langtry. Kathryn Wickum, the teacher, is seated on the steps, Boye and Buster Babb are at left, and the boy at far right is Arthur Torres. (Photo courtesy of Myrtle Babb Cash.)

Several members of the U.S. Cavalry stationed at Camp Langtry carved their names on a rock hill near the Rio Grande. A. Bunger was in Company C of the Third Calvalry.

duty at Camp Langtry usually lasted from two to four months. The camp was located at the edge of town and overlooked the Rio Grande and Crack Canyon.

Some of the troopers found time to carve their names or initials on a rock hill between the camp and the river. Some of the carved names that still remain legible after more than a hundred years are A. Bunger, A. Bonner, Konrad, W. Stanford, G. Murry, and Spann. Sergeant August Bunger, of Company C, Third Cavalry, was stationed at Camp Langtry during February 1887, but by July 1888, when he carved his name on the rock, he had been demoted to the rank of private.[4]

The main business establishments in Langtry just before the turn of the century were the J. P. Torres Store and Saloon, Roy Bean's Jersey Lilly Saloon, the Upshaw General Mercantile, the post office, located in the front room of the Fielder residence across the railroad from the depot, and the Pablo Cruz store, on the western edge of town.

Lumber that had to be brought in on the railroad was expensive, and Upshaw built his store of wooden grocery cases. After Upshaw was killed by Sam Bean (see pp. 21-24, Chapter 1) his wife sold the store to W. H. Dodd, and in later years, Dodd built an imposing building on the same site. All types of general ranch and household supplies were stocked in the W. H. Dodd Mercantile, but there were no facilities for keeping perishables. For his personal use, Dodd hung beef and deer in an adobe storeroom. In an interview, Cross Dodd told me his father would hang meat up in the storeroom, and it would get a crust on it and keep all winter.[5]

The people who lived at Langtry were tough. Shootings were not uncommon—and trouble was not limited to men. Cross Dodd told me about a ruckus between women:

> Mrs. Burdwell lived back up the hill a'ways from the operator's house, and she had a hen with some little chickens. There was an operator at Langtry whose wife had a cat, and one day that cat came up there trying to get the little chickens, so Mrs. Burdwell shot the cat.
>
> Mrs. Burdwell was a good woman, but she was pretty tough, and she wouldn't take nothing off nobody. She knew what to do with that cat. She took the dead cat back to that woman, and threw it down on her porch, and said, "Here's your damn cat. It killed two of my chickens."
>
> Boy, I'll tell you, that old lady Gardner really got sore and raised the dickens.[6]

Beula Burdwell Farley, like her mother, found early Langtry to be exciting:

> Langtry was a big place, and most of the activities of the town centered around the depot. There was lots of freight that used to come in to Langtry. Everything came in on the train, and most of it was in barrels. Flour came in barrels, sugar came in barrels, apples came in barrels, and a lot of other food did too. The depot was a busy place, and oh, that agent used to work hard. He worked a twelve-hour shift and then the night operator worked for twelve hours.
>
> There was a big eating house on one end of the depot, and at one time it was called the Cress News. It was later called the Brown News. It was a big place and had the biggest kitchen I ever saw.

The sink in that kitchen was the first sink I ever saw. I didn't even know there was such a thing as a kitchen sink before that. This one was made of tin, and I thought it was about the fanciest thing I had ever seen. The eating house was a lovely place, and I don't know how many rooms there were in the place, but there was a big dining room. Joining the dining room, there were two rooms where the people that worked there lived.

Every railroad crew ate there going and coming. There were also several railroad work gangs stationed at Langtry. Oh, Langtry was an exciting place.[7]

Roy Bean—School Trustee

By 1900, a school had been built in Langtry and an effort was being made to introduce the three R's to most of the area children. The school was a one-room frame house located west of the pumper's house. Roy Bean was one of the school trustees, and Beula Burdwell Farley recalled the judge's interest in the school:

When I really knew Judge Roy Bean, I was going to school and he was our trustee. He seen after our school. He seen after the money for the school and tried to keep the school open six months a year. Roy Bean would come up to the school every so often, and he would talk to the teacher, and he would be sure there was wood for the school.

We never had more than six months of school, and it was hard for our folks to keep us in school that long. We had to buy our own textbooks, and oh, they were high. I remember how my books came to six dollars one time, and my folks were poor. We were regular peddlers, that's what we were. Mama ran a dairy and brought milk and stuff to town to sell, and six dollars for one child was an awful lot of money to us.

I think they paid the teacher fifty dollars a month, and it was hard to get teachers. I tell you what kind of teachers we got—they weren't . . . them poor things. If you had been through the eighth grade, you would take your exam at the county judge's office in Del Rio, and if you passed the test, then you would get the first-grade certificate and maybe you would get the second.

The Brittains lived in Langtry, and Cary Brittain had been through about the eighth grade, and she decided she wanted to be a teacher. Judge Bean told her that if she could pass the exam, she could teach school in Langtry.

Carey went to Del Rio on the train with her brother and she passed the exam and came back and taught school at Langtry. They only had enough money to run a five-month school that year, so she had a pay-school and Mama paid a dollar and a half apiece for a month for each of us kids. That was for a whole month, and we was there five days a week.[8]

The school at Langtry was not much of a school in comparison with many others, but the folks at Langtry were proud of it. Many of the adults in the community could not read and write, and they were glad their children were getting the opportunity to learn.

Miss Winnie Elkins was one of the first teachers in Langtry. She signed her contract to teach school on September 9, 1901 and agreed to teach for five months for a salary of $35 per school month. It was also agreed that $1 per month would be charged for pupils under scholastic age and $1.50 per month for pupils over scholastic age—that amount, when collected, being paid to Miss Elkins. The contract was signed by Roy Bean and Cortez S. Fielder, trustees.

Lillie Langtry

Miss Elkins was still teaching in Langtry on January 4, 1904, when town and school were visited by actress Lillie Langtry. Everybody knew about Lillie Langtry, the beautiful and world-famous Jersey Lilly for whom Roy Bean had named his saloon. Bean—by this time deceased—had claimed he named the town in her honor.

Langtry was traveling in her own private railway coach, which was attached to the regular passenger train from New Orleans to San Francisco. The Southern Pacific arranged for the Sunset Limited to stop in Langtry longer than usual, so the actress could visit the town she thought was named for her. Shortly after the train stopped in front of the depot, Langtry stepped out to the rear platform of the observation car and was greeted by just about everyone who lived in the Langtry area. Miss Elkins and her school children were there. The women of the town wore their finest dresses, and most of

Although recent questions regarding its authenticity have caused it to be removed from display in the Jersey Museums, this silver-plated pistol, engraved for presentation to Lillie Langtry following her visit to the town of Langtry, was for many years thought to be Roy Bean's. Perhaps part of the controversy stems from the discrepancy between the inscription "Presented to 'Jersey Lily' Miss Lily Langtry from the townspeople of Langtry Texas 1903" in the photograph above and the much longer inscription that Langtry herself quotes in her book *The Days I Knew* (see page 174, this chapter). (Photo courtesy of Jersey Museums Service.)

the men wore dress shirts. A snare drummer and a horn blower produced some music as the actress stepped out of the train.

W. H. Dodd—who was himself English-born—greeted Langtry and presented the late Judge Bean's best pistol to her as a gift from the people of Langtry. Then Laura Torres, daughter of J. P. Torres and one of the more accomplished students in school, made a welcoming speech.

Rosa Babb Stapp was there, as a schoolgirl, and she remembered it as a great occasion:

> Lillie Langtry was a red-headed woman and rather large. She had a pretty face on her, and of course, she was all dressed up. Roy Bean had died about a year before, but Mrs. Langtry wanted to see his saloon. After the welcoming speech, she walked up to see the

English actress Lillie Langtry, for whom Judge Bean claimed he named the town of Langtry. She visited Langtry in 1904. (Photo courtesy of Jersey Museums Service.)

Dillard, Laura, Boye, and Buster Babb about 1906 on the front porch of the Opera House, where the Babb family lived after Roy Bean died. (Photo courtesy of Rosa Babb Stapp.)

Jersey Lilly, and there she was given some poker chips that had belonged to the old judge, and then she started on up to the schoolhouse.

Daddy had an old bear tied up there by our house, and as they walked from the saloon to the schoolhouse, they came right by our house, and they showed the bear to Lillie Langtry. It was our pet bear, and we had to take it into town while we were in school so we could feed it.

We had a pair of bears that my brother, John, had caught. He was always hunting with some hounds, and the dogs treed two cubs, and John climbed up the tree and caught them. We kept them until they got grown. We called one of them Ol' Purty, and she ate a cracked buckeye and it killed her. We kept the other one for the longest—and I hated that bear. I've got the scar on my arm today, where he bit me. I put the feed down in front of him one day, and he grabbed my arm. He didn't aim to hurt me, but he sure bit me.

Miss Winnie Elkins was teaching school at Langtry at the time of the visit by the famous actress, and when Miss Langtry discovered that the school building was too small to adequately take care of the students, she gave fifty dollars to use toward the enlargement of the school. The schoolhouse had only one room, so the money was used to make the building longer.[9]

The Sunset Limited had to move on and make up some of the time it had lost at Langtry, so Lillie Langtry was rushed back to the train. She waved good-bye to the crowd from the observation platform as the train chugged out of town, headed for San Francisco. Dodd retrieved Roy Bean's pistol from Langtry before she left, so he could have it engraved with a message for her. He later sent it to her, and subsequuently received a letter in reply, postmarked January 14, 1904:

As I wired you earlier, I have received Roy Bean's revolver and it will be forever treasured by me and mine, & now the box of resurrection plants has come. Indeed I thank you most heartily for all your kindness and hospitality which I never shall forget. I shall be so interested in the future of Langtry and I hope it will go on thriving & that I shall soon see you again for I feel I have friends in my name city.[10]

Years later, Lillie Langtry described her visit romantically in her book *The Days I Knew:*

Ambrose Burdwell and Willie Shaw in front of the Opera House with the hide of a mountain lion killed across the river from Langtry. They sold the hide to a railroad man for eight dollars—a big price in 1905. The hide had just been removed from the north side of the Jersey Lilly Saloon, where they had stretched it to dry. (Photo courtesy of Willie Shaw.)

The greatest surprise of all was to have a town named in my honour! . . . I received a letter from the founder [of the town—Roy Bean] pressing me to visit it. It was at the moment impossible, and on writing him my regrets, I offered to present an ornamental drinking fountain as a sop; but Roy Bean's quick reply was that it would be quite useless, as the only thing the citizens of Langtry did not drink was water. . . .

On a later trip to California by the southern route, the invitation was repeated by the "bigwigs" of the township, who besought me to take advantage of passing through Langtry to bestow half an hour on a reception. The Southern Pacific was willing. . . .

Justice of the Peace Dodd, a quiet, interesting man, introduced himself, and then presented Postmaster Fielding, Stationmaster Smith, and other persons of consequence. Next in order came a number of cowboys who were also formally introduced. Langtry did not boast a newspaper, and therefore these young men had gathered in from the ranges by means of mounted messengers. They were all garbed in their finest leathers and most flamboyant shirts, as became the occasion, making a picturesque group, one loosing off his gun as he passed me, in tangible proof of his appreciation of my visit.

Thirty or forty girls, all about fifteen or sixteen, followed, and were announced *en bloc* as "the young ladies of Langtry." And finally "our wives" brought up the rear. Justice Dodd then welcomed me in an apt speech, and after recounting the history of the town from its inception, declared that it would have been the proudest day in the late "King" Bean's life (he had been dead only a few months) if he had lived to meet me, adding, with obvious embarrassment, that his eldest son, aged twenty-one, who had been cast for the leading role in this unique reception, had received a sudden summons to San Francisco on important business. But it was generally whispered that he had taken fright at the prospect of the responsible part he was to play, and was lying in hiding somewhere among the universal sage brush. . . . The Jersey Lily Saloon was near at hand and we trudged to it through sage-brush and prickly cactus.

Boye Babb, Ambrose Burdwell, Jim Burdwell, and Willie Shaw show off their ropes in front of the Jersey Lily in 1906. (Photo courtesy of Willie Shaw.)

Langtry residents on the main street, Torres Avenue, about 1905. From left: Ada Upshaw, Laura Babb Tippett, Aaron Billings, Beula Burdwell, Gladys Raily, Laura Torres, Myrtle Cash (in front), Rosa Babb, Andrew Billings, Maude Babb Bates, four unidentified adults, Grandma Wall (big hat), Corder, Zeno Fielder, several unidentified adults, Mrs. Bill Ike Babb (with bonnet), Will Coleman (hat and black vest), Mr. Cup, or Bee Bee (in white hat), Charley Upshaw, Charles Upshaw (holding baby), Tom Conniff, W. H. Dodd, an unidentified adult, Mr. Coleman (with apron), Jerry Coleman (boy), Will Coleman (big black hat), Frank Coleman, Earl Coleman, Roy Coleman. The tree at right later became known as the Hanging Tree. (Photo and identification courtesy of Myrtle Babb Cash.)

I found it a roughly built wooden two-story house, its entire front being shaded by a piazza, on which a chained monkey gamboled, the latter (installed when the saloon was built) bearing the name of "The Lily" in my honour. The interiour of the "Ritz" of Langtry consisted of a long, narrow room, which comprised the entire ground floor, whence a ladder staircase led to a sleeping-loft. One side of the room was given up to a bar, naturally the most important feature of the place—while stoutly made tables and a few benches occupied the vacant space. The tables showed plainly that they had been severely used, for they were slashed as of with bowie-knives and on each was a well-thumbed deck of playing cards. It was here that Roy Bean, Justice Of The Peace, and self-styled "law west of the Pecos River" used to hold his court and administer justice . . . .

We still had a few minutes to see the schoolhouse, which was adjacent to the saloon, but the schoolmistress had sensibly locked the door on this great holiday, so after pledging myself to send a supply of suitable books from San Francisco, I returned to the train. The cemetery was pointed out to me in the distance, and the significant fact deduced that only fifteen of the citizens buried there had died natural deaths. . . .

On nearing the train, which was becoming rather impatient, I saw the strange sight of a huge cinnamon bear careering across the line, dragging a cowboy at the end of a long chain. . . . On my journey through the south I had acquired a jumping frog at Charlston, an alligator in Florida, a number of horned toads, and a delightingly tame prairie dog called Bod. Hence, I suppose, the correct inference was drawn that I was fond of animals, and the boys resolved to add the late Roy Bean's pet to my collection. They hoisted the unwilling animal on to the platform, and tethered him to the rail, but happily, before I had time to rid myself of this unwelcome addition without seeming discourteous, he broke away, scattering the crowd and causing some of the vaqueros to start shooting wildly at all angles.

It was a short visit, but an unforgettable one. As a substitute for the runaway bear, I was presented later with Roy Bean's revolver, which . . . bears the following inscription: "Presented by W. H. Dodd, of Langtry, Texas to Mrs. Lillie Langtry in honour of her visit to our town. This pistol was formerly the property of Judge Roy Bean. It aided him in finding some of his famous decisions and keeping order west of the Pecos River. It also kept order in the Jersey Lily Saloon. Kindly accept this as a small token of our regards."[11]

Langtry's account ended with mention of another gift: a box of resurrection-plants from the desert—which, sold in cities, were "one of the sources of revenue to Langtry." She said she gave one to the American painter, John S. Sargent.

It was about the time of the Langtry visit that the Jersey Lilly saloon closed. After Bean's death, Bill Ike Babb bought the saloon and the Opera House from Bean's heirs. He hired Tom Coniff, a young man who had moved west to cure his tuberculosis, to run the saloon. Bob Bates also ran the saloon for a short time for Babb, but with Roy Bean gone, the saloon was no longer a success. When the liquor license that had been issued to Bean expired, Bill Ike Babb closed the saloon. He needed some lumber at the ranch, so he tore down the billiard hall that was attached to the saloon. Reportedly, Mrs. Babb made him quit tearing down the building, because she felt that some day people would be coming to Langtry to see the Jersey Lilly Saloon.[12]

Mapped by Marshall

After Bean died, Langtry continued to thrive, but it was still a primitive town, sixty miles from a doctor. General George C. Marshall—who later, during World War II, became chief of staff of the U.S. Army and later still, secretary of state—endured hardships of the Langtry area.

In 1905, then Lieutenant Marshall was assigned to make a map of western Val Verde County. He traveled by train to Fort Clark, where he was supplied with a sergeant to assist him, a packer with twenty mules, a cook, and an escort wagon with a four-line mule team. His primary source of food for men and mules was Langtry.

While surveying from Comstock to Langtry, Marshall recalled that his thermometer would go up to 130 degrees F as he walked along counting the sections of rails for an exact measurement of distance. Marshall and his crew reached Langtry at the end of July, and he was cheered at the prospect of picking up his pay there and being able to buy food. His sergeant had had only water to drink for a month, so he drew his pay and found a house with girls and bottles and settled in. The sergeant announced that the girls were all for him and declared the place off limits to everyone else. Marshall soon heard his helper was causing a problem in the community, so he talked the sergeant into agreeing to share his domain and drink in peace, which he did as long as his pay lasted.

Marshall completed his mapping of the area in late August and later, according to a biographer, described it as "the hardest service I ever had in the Army." He had gone into the area weighing 170 pounds and came out weighing 132 pounds.[13]

Marshall found the little frontier town to be lacking in many of the conveniences he was accustomed to. My father, Guy Skiles, remembered how people had to do the best they could with what they had:

> I remember when we were living in Langtry in 1911, an old Mexican by the name of Marcos had a ranch on the Pecos, and he came in on the train sick. They carried him off the train and laid him up there against the depot and tried to doctor him, but he died.
>
> They got an undertaker up there from Del Rio to embalm him, and several of us kids stood around and watched the undertaker embalm him on the front porch of the old Fielder house, which was also the post office. People were accustomed to the raw facts of life and nobody seemed to be bothered about them embalming that fellow on the porch of the post office.[14]

A Rip-Roarin' Town

Langtry was a rip-roaring town for many years. Until long after 1900, most of the men would never leave home without their six-shooters—and Beula Burdwell Farley described one incident to me that showed they did so with reason:

> Graham Barnett killed Will Babb on Monday, the eighth day of December, 1913. Graham Barnett and Reid House were working for Joe Graham, but they came in to Langtry to help my husband, Buck Billings. Buck was working cattle at Eight Mile on the Pecos, and he hired these boys to help him.
>
> We were living in a house on the main street of Langtry about a block down the street from the Torres house. It belonged to Mrs.

Dodd and we were renting it for ten dollars a month. Will Babb was living in the Opera House and he and his wife had a baby two weeks old, and she also had two other children.

Buck and Graham and Reid finished working cattle that Sunday about noon and come on in to Langtry, and Graham and Reid spent the night with us. The next morning Buck asked me if I had any blank checks so he could pay off the boys, and I told him no. He said he would go up to Mr. Dodd's store with the boys and get a check cashed there and pay them.

Buck went on up to the store to pay the boys, but he didn't have his six-shooter on. He just never went anywhere without his six-shooter, but he went off and left it under his pillow that morning. The three men went on up to Mr. Dodd's, and after a little bit, I looked out the window and old Reid House was running one of our gentle saddle horses around and around in our horse pen. He had a bridle in his hand and was trying to catch that horse. He was all excited and John Babb's wife, who lived across the street from us, and I ran out to the horse pen about the same time to see what was wrong.

Reid turned towards us and said, "Graham shot Will Babb."

I don't remember what Lucy, that's John Babb's wife, said, but she hung on the fence for a minute.

I said, "Reid, did he kill him?"

Reid said. "He's very dead."

Directly, here comes Buck, after his gun, and I said, "Buck, what's wrong? What happened?"

It seems that Graham and Will had gotten in some sort of an argument over a mule. He said Will had gotten his pocketknife out and had raked Graham across the chest with it. Will had apparently seen murder in Graham's eye, so he closed his knife and got it about halfway into his pocket when Graham shot him. Will was one-eyed and Graham shot him right under the good eye. When he did, Graham turned around and John Babb was standing right beside him. Graham threw the gun down on John, and John said, "Why Graham, I'm ashamed of you."

All this was taking place in front of Mr. Dodd's store. I think Ike Billings was a constable, or something. Anyway Buck and Graham went over to Ike's house. Now this happened about nine o'clock in the morning. Graham had given up and they had already decided to take him to Del Rio on the train. The train ran at eleven-o-five so they didn't have much time. They wanted to get Graham out of town because they were afraid some of the Babbs might get upset and try to kill him for what he had done to Will.

Ike Billings, and Buck and Graham Barnett, and Joe Graham [Graham Barnett's uncle] all caught the train and went to Del Rio and they hired Walter Gillis, Joe Jones, and Thurmond for lawyers— and they were good ones. They were the best durn' lawyers you ever saw. When old man Thurmond got a case, he would get up in front of a jury and just cry his eyes out and have everybody feeling sorry for him.

They moved the trial to Fort Stockton and Graham Barnett came clear as a whistle, because of his and his family's reputation of being good citizens—but it ruined him. He got mean and got to where he just killed for the fun of it. He had been a nice boy before that happened, but he got to be a regular murderer.[15]

Another killing occurred in Jesus Torres's saloon on the main street of Langtry. Manuel Terrazas worked for W. H. Dodd for a number of years and was well liked by most of the townspeople. Manuel's wife was named Martina, and they lived in a small house that Dodd had built for them behind the Dodd store. Manuel did chores for Dodd, and one of his duties was to carry freight in a two-wheeled cart from the depot to the store. He also milked a cow for Dodd; each morning and evening he took a bucket of milk to the Dodd house and left it on the back porch. Cross Dodd told:

One evening Manuel did not show up to do his chores, and Dad assumed that Manuel was across the street at the Torres Saloon so he sent me over to get Manuel.

When I got to the front porch of the saloon, old Manuel was laying out there dead. I ran home and told Dad that Manuel was dead, and then Dad went over to take charge of Manuel's body and find out what had happened. I think a fellow named Metz, who was an operator on the railroad, had shot him.[16]

At the time of the shooting, Jesus Torres was staying alone in his combination home and saloon; his wife was in San Antonio visiting relatives. There were four rooms in the house and one was quite large, serving as store and saloon. After the shooting had stopped, Jesus Torres could not be found, so the men proceeded to search through and around the house for him. It was thought that he might have been hit by a stray bullet. As the men searched the house, one of them noticed a boot sticking out from under a bed: Torres was hiding under the bed, afraid he, too, might get shot.

Manuel Terrazas was buried in the cemetery at Langtry, but no tombstone was erected to mark his grave.

Charlie Small

One of the more colorful characters, whose remains also rest unmarked in the cemetery overlooking the Rio Grande a short distance west of Langtry, was Charlie Small, a friend of Roy Bean's. Bandits from Mexico frequently crossed the Rio Grande and raided settlers prior to 1900. It was understood by some of the folks living along the border that Charlie Small's family had been killed by some of these bandits, and that Small had vowed to spend the rest of his life getting even with raiders from Mexico. Small spent his time roaming around the country north of the Rio Grande and gained a reputation, primarily among Anglos living in the area, as a sort of Robin Hood figure. He was well known and frequently dropped in on settlers and cowboy camps and stayed a few days.

In reminiscences printed in the *Frontier Times*, Bob Beverly gave a sense of Small's lifestyle. Beverly was near the mouth of the Pecos when he first met the legendary Small:

> One day there rode up to this hangout a man I sure liked the looks of. I thought if he had been up in the northwestern states he would have put a lot of those rustlers there on the run. He was riding the finest Mexican saddle, on as good a horse as I ever saw in the Rio Grande country at that time, and he wore a large Mexican sombrero, covered with silver around the band and along the brim. I sure fell for him. He had plenty of 'dobe dollars, and though they were cheap, he made them look cheaper the way he gambled them off. And say, I fell for this guy's talk, and but few if any of the

crowd gave him any back talk, and me, I was his slave; I craved his good will.

I noticed that the copper-colored fellows all took to the hills and brush in about ten minutes from the time this fellow showed up, and there were several around that had guns with notches filed on the handles who had nothing out of the way to say to this gent.

Joe Sitters, afterwards killed, as river guard in the Big Bend country, at that time had just made a run with the Texas Rangers after the Sanderson train robbers, and helped to round them up above the Ozona country, near the old High Lonesome ranch of Heard & White, was around Comstock and Langtry at that time, and several different kinds of officers would drop by every few days to water at the tent.

But this man I looked upon as one of the most daring gunmen I had ever run on to. He drank moderately not too much, played cards and gambled above board. At times he would throw in a handful of dollars, saying "I took them dollars off of a rural rider on the other side of the river, and I will get more over there when I run out," and everybody would laugh.

I asked Uncle Mack, the old man I was lined up with, who this gentleman was. "Oh," he said, "That is the man Texas and Mexico had trouble over, and Texas made Mexico turn him loose. He is all right, kid. Treat him right and he will be a friend to you when you need one. His name is Charlie Small."

He told me he was in Old Mexico, and got into some trouble down there to begin with, and they sentenced him for life to dig salt down under ground. They would take him out a lot of mornings and whip him across the back and then rub salt into the lash wounds. Finally his people and some of his friends got Sul Ross, the Governor, to make the Mexican government turn him loose. They brought him to this side of the border and released him with the warning to never cross the border into Mexico again. I said, "Did you ever go back on the other side?" He looked at me a long time and said, "I was over there today, and I emptied my gun into one or two and as long as I live I aim to do the same way."

I learned that if a Mex killed a man on this side of the border, the ranchers along there would give Charlie Small his number, and sooner or later he would come along and tell the ranchers how it happened on the other side of the border, usually giving over something that the hombre had taken from the man he had killed on this side, like the case I knew of the herders killing John Otto, sheepman working for Igner west of Cow Creek, and fled across the Rio Grande. Charlie Small even brought back part of John's clothing, and I think his horse, and that was all there was to it.

During the winter of 1892, some Mexicans came over to Comstock one night and robbed Amed & Jennings' store, taking quilts and packed two horses with goods out of the store and tied quilts around the goods. They killed old Scar Faced Charlie, and crossed back into Mexico. Joe Sitters and the customs man followed the trail, and I went along, for several days over across the river to see if we could overtake them. When we would get to where it was brush we would see little pieces of red cloth hanging on limbs of the brush, and we could ride along like we were going to church, no trouble to trace the way they went.

A short time after that Charlie Small came and told me he beat us to the hombres. I do not know, but he did a good job if he did do it. Old Scar Faced Charlie had fed Small many a night when the Texas Rangers were crowding Small. Of course he got in bad on this side of the river, after he went over and back to the other side on many missions of death, and the Rangers hunted him a lot of times praying they would not find him. For after all, Charlie Small had taken a lot of trouble off the hands of the Rangers and sheriffs along the Rio Grande, for most of the men he went across on the other side to hunt to death got what was due them, and this saved the officers along the border on this side a lot of ammunition.[17]

As well as being a friend of Roy Bean's and of other folks at Langtry, Small frequently called on a widow of the community. One evening he called on the widow, who lived in a small house on the side of the hill north of the railroad water tank, nearing sundown. Small walked with the young lady down the hill toward the center of town. Just after the couple walked past the water tank, Small was shot in the back and killed. It was believed generally that a ranger, who Langtry folks later said wanted to make a name for himself, had been hiding near the water tank and ambushed Small as he walked by.

The ranger quickly left town, and Small was buried in the graveyard on the west side of Langtry. The tough man of the border had been in love with the young woman, and for many years, the Langtry folks were reminded of that love when they went down to the banks of the Rio Grande and saw where Small had carved his name and the name of the woman on a big hackberry tree beside the trail.

Across the River

There has never been any settlement on the Rio Grande opposite Langtry, but, during the Mexican Revolution, between two and three hundred Carranzistas (followers of Venustiano Carranza) were camped for a few months on the big flat above the eagle nest. Harvey Hall remembered that time. Hall had come to Langtry as a railroad telegraph operator in 1911 (he married Dorothy Dodd, daughter of W. H. and Lulu Dodd in 1919). When I interviewed him in 1963, his memories of the Mexican soldiers were still vivid:

> During this time those fellows over there had no ammunition, and Mr. Dodd got it for them. There was a customs officer at Langtry then, but the Mexicans could take food and clothing across the river. They were not allowed to take other things such as arms and ammunition across, though.
>
> Of course the Mexicans sure liked peanuts, so they would come to the store and buy a big bag of peanuts. Mr. Dodd would put a big handful of thirty-thirty cartridges in the bottom of the sack and a bunch of peanuts on top. The Mexicans would come out of the store and walk down the street toward the river eating peanuts and go on across the river. Two or three hundred of those Mexicans making a couple of trips each across the river soon had enough ammunition to do some good with.
>
> Mr. Dodd got two old, water-cooled machine guns, and sold them to the general. The commander was supposed to know all about them, but I don't think he did, because they had too much trouble with them.
>
> Some of the men associated with the army camp, mainly officers, stayed over on this side of the river in the roominghouse. I was staying in the roominghouse and became friendly with them. They had

no place to go, and I worked as a telegraph operator, so they would come up to the depot and sit around and talk to me.

The officers, like most Mexican officers, were of the ruling class of people in Mexico. They were well-to-do people, which was the reason they were officers. Most of the officers I knew were gentlemen, had good appearance, and were high-class Mexicans.[18]

Simon Shaw, Jr., also remembered the Mexican soldiers who crossed the border to Langtry:

The Mexican officers stayed at the hotel at Langtry, and there was lots of business transacted there at Langtry at that time. Trav Brown was telling about one time he came in the hotel to deliver a message to one of the Mexicans. A Mexican was laying up on the bed drunk and had about $50,000 there laying beside the bed. Trav could have taken it and the Mexican never known about it, but he didn't touch it. It was payday, and the money was to pay off the men across the river. I guess there were about two hundred men camped across the river then.[19]

At one time while the Carranzistas were camped across the river from Langtry, a force of men loyal to Pancho Villa came close to their camp and a skirmish between the two groups resulted. The gunshots could be heard at Langtry and much of the population of the town gathered at the top of the bluff on the U.S. side of the river to watch the activity. The small detachment of Pancho Villa's men fled quickly when they realized how many of Carranza's men were in the area. After the exchange, the soldiers loyal to Carranza obtained short pieces of three-inch pipe and loaded them with dynamite and bolts to serve as land mines. Some of the crude mines were left in the ground opposite Langtry and were not found until years later.

Following the skirmish, the people of Langtry became increasingly nervous. On May 8, 1916, postmaster W. H. Dodd sent a letter to General Frederick Funston: "In view of the recent raids and the exposed condition of our town I have been requested by the citizens to call on you for more troops for our protection. We now have eighteen soldiers who are here protecting the railroad for the passage of troops and that leaves our families and children at the mercy of any raiding band. Our town can be shot up from the Mexican side or attacked on the Texas side. Give us protection if possible."[20] It is not known how successful the request for reinforcements was, but the threat of invasion from Mexico diminished and life at Langtry became more routine. Soldiers moved out of the barracks buildings located on railroad property near the community park, and railroad employees moved into the buildings.

Bootlegging

When the Mexican Revolution was over, things settled down in Langtry for a few years. Then prohibition came into effect. There was plenty of liquor in Mexico, and it was easily smuggled across the Rio Grande. A large number of law-enforcement men were stationed along the border with Mexico in an effort to stop or control smuggling. One of the most colorful of the old-time peace officers along the border was Captain W. L. Barler, a former captain of the Texas Rangers. For many years after his service in the rangers, Barler—or Cap, as he was known—served as a U.S. Customs officer assigned to the lower trans-Pecos to apprehend smugglers. His job was a tough one: he was attempting to watch more than a hundred miles of the roughest border country and liquor was being crossed almost everywhere.

A number of active bootleggers lived in Langtry. One of them, an old man who lived on the eastern edge of town, near Crack Canyon, had built a small adobe house in the middle of a large area of nearly flat, solid rock; consequently, he did not have to build a floor for his home. Near the adobe house, the man built a large adobe oven, typical of the type used in Mexico, and he baked bread and sold it to the people of Langtry. Being a baker, his name seemed to become lost and folks just called him Panadero, from the Spanish word for *baker*.

Old Panadero was a sly smuggler and none of the lawmen could catch him doing anything illegal, although they all knew that he made most of his meager living by selling smuggled whiskey. Cap Barler laid out in the bushes near Panadero's house on several occasions in attempts to catch him transporting whiskey, but was never able to get the goods on the old baker.

Finally one day, a local informer told Barler he would fill him in on where old Panadero kept his liquor hidden. Barler was eager to get the information, and quickly encouraged him. The informer directed the officer to go over close to Crack Canyon, to Panadero's chicken house, where he would find Panadero's whiskey buried inside. Anxious to nail Panadero, Cap rustled around, borrowed a pick and shovel, and got a couple of men to help him dig up the cache. The trio then proceeded down to Panadero's house and found the old baker at home.

Panadero was friendly and cordial, as usual, but of course figured something was up when he saw the men carrying the pick and shovel. Cap Barler asked Panadero where his chicken house was, and the old fellow pointed toward the little shack between his house and Crack Canyon. With his pick and shovel men in tow, Barler marched out to the chicken house and opened the door. To his dismay and disgust he found that the floor of the chicken house was solid rock. The informer had played a joke on Cap, but the tough old former ranger captain did not find one thing funny about it.

Barler was a typical Texas Ranger, and it was not often that anyone got the best of him. He stopped a lot of smuggling along the river. One account tells of an attempt he thwarted about a half mile down the river from Langtry.

Cap and another customs officer, Charley McBee, suspected some activity at the mouth of Eagle Nest Canyon one day, so they hid between some rocks on top of the bluff on the east side of the canyon, where it runs into the Rio Grande. They watched quietly as a man came out of the bushes on the Mexican side of the river carrying a washtub with several bottles of whiskey in it. The man waded across the river, floating the tub beside him, and as he neared the U.S. side of the river, a man stepped out of the brush to meet him. Barler told McBee to watch the men from the top of the bluff and cover him while he slipped down into the vega to arrest the men. Before he could get to the river, the men had concluded the deal, and the American had put the bottles of whiskey in a burlap sack.

The Mexican started back across the river with his newly earned money and some tobacco in the tub. Barler stepped out of the brush and told the men to hold it, and as he showed himself, some Mexicans on the bluff on the other side of the river started shooting at him. Barler and McBee returned the fire, and while they were thus busy, the smuggler abandoned his tub in the river and scrambled back into Mexico. The lawmen apprehended the American smuggler, and a few days later the tub was found washed up on a gravel bar down the river with $20 and three cans of tobacco in it.

The man who brought the whiskey to the river was probably Guerro Taniz, for whom the vega opposite Twin Caves was named. He lived in a cave above the lower end of Taniz Vega and was a known bootlegger.[21]

The constable at Langtry during prohibition times was Bart Gobble. Although he did not agree with the idea of prohibition, it was his duty to enforce the law. Robert Gatlin told me that one time Gobble got word that a man had some liquor, so he watched the man and caught him at the stock pens with a couple of bottles of whiskey. Gobble felt sorry for the old fellow, a Mexican, but told him he would have to arrest him. They knew each other well, so they sat down beside the stock pens to discuss the problem and the Mexican offered Gobble a drink. After talking over the problem at length, Gobble held up the two bottles that he and the Mexican had drunk from and told the old fellow that he couldn't arrest him, because the bottles were empty and there was no evidence.[22]

Gatlin also told of a confrontation between Cap Barler and Bart Gobbles:

Captain Barler knew that Bart Gobbles not only failed to enforce the prohibition laws, but he also did some smuggling himself. Bart was sitting by the stove in the Dodd Store one day, when Captain Barler came walking in. Cap got after Bart about bootlegging whiskey and told him what all he was going to do if he caught him at it.

Bart listened to all the threats that Cap made and when he got through, Bart said, "If you're gonna do all that, then I'm not gonna let you catch me."[23]

A Tragedy

Langtry experienced its greatest tragedy on February 22, 1925, when an explosion at the railroad's steam-driven rock crusher, about one mile west of town, killed eight men and injured several others. About every three months, a large slice of rock on the hill at the quarry was blasted off to provide material for the crusher. A well-drilling rig was used to drill fifty or more holes, and these were loaded with dynamite and blasting powder to blast out the rock.

On the day of the blast, Rufus Kessler, who had moved to Langtry only the year before, was working as a fireman in the engine room that supplied power to the rock-crushing machinery. He described the scene at the quarry the morning of the blast:

About eight o'clock, I walked up on the quarry floor from the back door of the engine room and stood there about twenty minutes, watching the laborers carrying boxes of dynamite and cans of powder up on the hill. From where I was watching these men, they

Rock crusher west of Langtry before the tragic explosion. The crusher provided ballast to hold railroad ties in place. (Photo courtesy of Antonio Zapata.)

reminded me of a long row of ants going and coming from their nests. I could hear them talking and some were singing.

As the dynamite and powder was carried up the hill, the required amount was placed at each hole. Around ten o'clock that morning, the dynamite, powder, caps, fuses, electric wiring, and other materials had been deposited around a large number of the drilled holes and some were already loaded.

About ten forty-five, George Scowan, the stationary engineer, and I heard a powerful explosion. We ran out the back door and up to the quarry floor. I could see dust and smoke, smell burned powder, and see men staggering around and hear them shouting.

I knew something terrible had happened on the hill and immediately shut down the steam engines and ran back to the quarry floor and started towards the top of the hill where the explosion had occurred. As I hit the climb at the foot of the hill, I encountered Pete Vincent staggering down the hill. His clothes were almost gone, his face was bleeding, and he hardly knew what was going on. I said, "My God, Pete, what happened?"

He said, "I don't know Rufus, but everyone was killed up there. Hurry on up."

When I arrived at the top of the hill, it was hard to believe what I saw. I quickly surveyed the situation and saw several bodies. My little dog had followed me and he immediately went over to Tom Dorris's body [the quarry superintendent], put his head straight up, howled three or four times, and left. So many people were in agony. I could see several injured going down the hill on the opposite side from where I came up. One of the dynamite holes was still smoking, and hands, feet, and burnt flesh were laying all around.[24]

A freight train heading toward Del Rio was summoned and three or four badly injured men were put in the caboose and taken to Del Rio. Five of the eight men killed in the explosion were buried in the Langtry cemetery the next day.

Railroad officials and men from the powder and dynamite companies investigated the accident, but no cause of the explosion could be determined. Some of the men speculated that a babbit tamper cast by superintendent Dorris the day before to tamp the powder in the holes might have caused a spark that set off the explosion.

New Growth

There was always a lot going on in Langtry, especially around the railroad. All the trains stopped for water and often unloaded freight at the depot, section crews were coming and going, and the operators at the depot were busy sending and receiving train orders in Morse code that were to be relayed to the train conductors.

During sheep shearing season, there were always sacks of wool in the warehouse end of the depot. If the kids of the community were not in school, they were often playing on the sacks of wool. The stock pens across from the depot and down the track were often busy places, as ranchers loaded lambs or occasionally calves or horses into railroad stock cars.

Throughout the Mexican Revolution and the prohibition era, Langtry had continued to prosper as a railroad town and ranching center. The W. H. Dodd General Mercantile, which opened on the main street of the town in 1895, was a center of activity for many years. Dodd sold groceries and ranch

Two of the U.S. Army soldiers stationed at Langtry in 1917–18 to protect the village from Mexican revolutionaries. They are standing in the main street. The hills in the background are in Mexico. (Photo courtesy of William Waldron.)

supplies and the U.S. post office was located in one corner of the building. Dodd also built a small hotel and a restaurant that his wife operated.

Pablo Cruz operated a grocery store on the west side of town, and Jimmy Merritt opened a general merchandise store behind the Opera House.

The first school building in Langtry, situated southwest of the Opera House, became too small and a larger one was built behind the Torres house. In 1911, a long, larger building was erected nearby. In 1935, a stucco building was erected that contained four large classrooms and an auditorium.

The Mother's Club, with help from railroad personnel, maintained a town park on railroad property between the Dodd store and the railroad tracks. Weather permitting, many of the Langtry residents gathered at the park in the evenings to play dominoes or croquet, to pitch horseshoes, watch the goldfish in the fountain, or play other games beneath the palm trees. Dances were frequently held on the concrete slab located at one corner of the park, and a large barbecue pit nearby was often covered with cabrito (barbecued goat meat).

The Hanging Tree in Langtry, 1955. The tree was never used to hang anyone, but drunken rowdies at town dances in the adjacent town park were handcuffed and chained to the tree until they sobered up. Roy Bean's saloon and Opera House are in the background.

Nearby, a large mesquite tree, growing in the middle of the main street at Dodd's store, served as the town jail. Lawbreakers were chained to the tree: most were drunks who had gotten too rowdy at the dance and were chained there until they sobered up. Although the tree later became known as the hanging tree, it was never used for that purpose.

The grassy park, a beautiful green oasis in the desert, thrived because water was free in Langtry. The railroad pumped a tremendous amount of clear spring water for the trains and let the townspeople use all they wanted. However, the railroad was destined to abandon the Langtry townsite. In 1925, the Southern Pacific began constructing a new roadbed north of Langtry that would shorten its route and eliminate bridges over Osman Canyon that occasionally washed out. A new depot and section houses were built about a mile north of town, and the main line soon bypassed Langtry. In June 1926, the old depot in front of the abandoned Jersey Lilly burned. Rails from the main line to the rock crusher west of town continued to go through Langtry, but when its building burned in 1929, the rock crusher was abandoned and the rails through the Langtry townsite were removed.

Langtry now seemed to be a hard-luck town. Then, in 1939, the Texas Highway Department built a loop road off U.S. 90, passing through the townsite in front of the Jersey Lilly exactly where the railroad had been a few years earlier. The highway department also restored Roy Bean's Jersey Lilly and Langtry became a tourist destination. Fittingly then, its seems, Judge Roy Bean, Law West of the Pecos, who helped found the town of Langtry, Texas, continues to keep it alive.

REFERENCES

Chapter 1, Judge Roy Bean

1. County Clerk's Office, Shelby County Courthouse, Shelbyville, Ky.
2. Major Horace Bell, *Reminiscences of a Ranger*, (Santa Barbara, Calif.: n.p., 1927).
3. Ibid.
4. *Las Cruces Citizen*, March 3, 1955.
5. Dorothy Watson, *The Pinos Altos Story*, (Silver City, N. Mex.: Print Shop, May 1978), p. 5.
6. St. Mary's University Bulletin, Vol. 6. No. 2, San Antonio, Tex., April 1973.
7. Vinton Lee James, *Frontier and Pioneer Recollections in San Antonio and West Texas* (San Antonio, Tex.: Artes Graficas Press, 1938), p. 76.
8. State Archives, Austin, Tex.
9. *San Antonio Express*, August 8, 1882.
10. Pecos County Records, Fort Stockton Courthouse, Fort Stockton, Tex.
11. Mary Waurine Hunter, "Windbag Law," *Texas Parade*, (October 1939), p. 527.
12. Southern Pacific Railroad records, Houston, Tex.
13. "Roy Bean, the 'Law West of the Pecos'," *El Paso Herald*, n.d. (1914).
14. Willie Shaw, interviewed by the author, Alpine, Tex., 1966.
15. Mrs. Beula Burdwell Farley, interviewed by the author, Sanderson, Tex., 1965.
16. Ibid.
17. Ibid.
18. Neal Billings, interviewed by the author, Langtry, Tex., 1970.
19. Willie Shaw interview, 1966.
20. Farley interview, 1965.
21. Cross Dodd, interviewed by the author, Austin, Tex., 1963.
22. Rosa Babb Stapp, interviewed by the author, Alpine, Tex., 1966.
23. George Curry, *George Curry, 1861–1947, An Autobiography*, edited by H. Henning (Albuquerque: Univ. of New Mexico Press, 1958), p. 60.
24. State Archives, Austin, Tex.
25. Allie Berry, interviewed by the author, Langtry, Tex., 1982.

Chapter 2, Explorers and Indian Fighters

1. Albert H. Schroeder and Dan Matson, *A Colony on the Move*, Gaspar Castano de Sosa's Journal, 1590–1591 (Salt Lake City: Alphabet Printing, 1965), pp. 39–51.
2. Castaneda, *Our Catholic Heritage*, Vol. II, (Austin, Tex.: Von Boeckmann-Jones, 1936), pp. 336–343.

3. William H. Emory, *Report on the United States and Mexican Boundary Survey*, Vol. I, Ch. V. (Washington, D.C.: Cornelious Wenderell, Printer, 1857), pp. 74–80.

4. Michler (who was under the command of Major Emory) wrote his comments in a report quoted by Emory in his survey.

5. Ibid.

6. Carl S. Raht, *The Romance Of Davis Mountains And Big Bend Country*, (Odessa, Tex.: Rahtbooks, 1963), p. 127.

7. Colonel M. L. Crimmins, "Colonel J. F. K. Mansfield's Inspection Report of Texas," *Southwestern Historical Quarterly*, Vol. LV, July, 1951, pp. 255–256.

8. August Santleben, *A Texas Pioneer* (New York & Washington, D.C.: Neal Publishing, 1910), p. 143–144.

9. Mrs. Beula Burdwell Farley, interviewed by the author, Sanderson, Tex., 1965.

10. See Kenneth Wiggins Porter, *Southwestern Historical Quarterly*, Volume LV, January 1952, No. 3, pp. 359–365.

11. See Edward S. Wallace, *Southwestern Historical Quarterly*, Vol. LV, July 1951, pp. 78–79.

12. Colonel M. L. Crimmins, "The Border Command—Camp Bullis," *Army and Navy Courier*, Nov. 1926, pp. 18–21.

13. Guy Skiles, interviewed by the author, Langtry, Tex., 1963.

14. See Edward S. Wallace, *Southwestern Historical Quarterly*, Vol. LV, July 1951 p. 82.

15. Ibid.

16. From a letter dated October 26, 1879 in the Texas Archives, Ranger Records, Austin, Tex.

17. Frost Woodhull, *Frontier Times*, December 1937, Vol. 15, No. 3, p. 120.

18. Frederick Remington, *Century Magazine*, July 1889.

Chapter 3, Building the Railroad

1. Quoted in J. Marvin Hunter, *The Trail Drivers of Texas*, 1925, p. 23.

2. Simon Shaw, Jr., interviewed by the author, Del Rio, Tex., 1964.

3. *San Antonio Daily Express*, August 5, 1882.

4. *San Antonio Daily Express*, April 23, 1882.

5. *San Antonio Daily Express*, June 27, 1882.

6. *San Antonio Daily Express*, December 13, 14, 15, and 19, 1882.

Chapter 4, Keeping the Trains Running

1. Homer Low, "Simon Shaw," a family manuscript in the possession of Dorothy Shaw Billings, Langtry, Tex.

2. *S. P. Bulletin*, August 1940, Vol. 24, No. 8, Southern Pacific Bureau of News, San Francisco, Calif.

3. Simon Shaw, Jr., interviewed by the author, Del Rio, Tex., 1964.

4. James McMullen, interviewed by Sam Woolford and quoted in the *San Antonio Light*, February 27, 1955, page 4-B.

5. See *El Paso Herald*, March 27, 1893.

6. W. H. McBee, interviewed by the author, Langtry, Tex., 1972.

7. Mrs. Allie Stidham Berry, interviewed by the author, Langtry, Tex., 1973.

8. See Nancy Alexander, *Father of Texas Geology, Robert T. Hill* (Dallas, Tex.: S.M.U. Press, 1976).

9. Mrs. Beulah Burdwell Farley, interviewed by the author, Sanderson, Tex., 1965.

10. Willie Shaw, interviewed by the author, Alpine, Tex., 1965.

11. Quoted in J. Marvin Hunter, "The Killing of Captain Frank Jones," *Frontier Times*, Vol. 6, No. 4, Jan., 1929, pp. 147–149 [paragraphing inserted].

12. Cross Dodd, interviewed by the author, Austin, Tex., 1963.

13. Willie Shaw interview, 1965.

Chapter 5, Squatting and Homesteading

1. R. J. Lauderdale and John M. Doak, *Life on the Range and on the Trail* (San Antonio, Tex.: Naylor Company, 1936).

2. Mrs. Beulah Burdwell Farley, interviewed by the author, Sanderson, Tex., 1965.

3. Mrs. Myrtle Babb Cash, interviewed by the author, Cash Ranch, Val Verde County, Tex., 1965.

4. Mrs. Rosa Babb Stapp, interviewed by the author, Alpine, Tex., 1965.

5. Henry Mills, Jr., interviewed by the author, Langtry, Tex., May 1991.

6. Farley interview, 1965.

7. Horace Shackelford, interviewed by the author, Langtry, Tex., April 1991.

8. Stapp interview, 1966.

9. Mrs. Lilly Burdwell Shelton, interviewed by the author, Shelton Ranch, Terrell County, Tex., 1965.

10. Cross Dodd, interviewed by the author, Austin, Tex., 1963.

11. Alfred Shelton, interviewed by the author, Shelton Ranch, Terrell County, Tex., 1965.

12. Guy Skiles, interviewed by the author, Langtry, Tex., 1974.

Chapter 6, Ranching

1. Mrs. Myrtle Babb Cash, interviewed by the author, Cash Ranch, Val Verde County, Tex., 1965.

2. Guy Skiles, interviewed by the author, Langtry, Tex., 1965.

3. Ibid.

4. Ibid.

5. Guy Skiles, interviewed by the author, Langtry, Tex., 1979.

6. Ibid.

7. Alfred Shelton, interviewed by the author, Shelton Ranch, Terrell County, Tex., 1965.

Chapter 7, Langtry

1. R. J. Lauderdale and John M. Doak, *Life on the Range and on the Trail*, (San Antonio, Tex.: Naylor, 1936).
2. Pecos County Deed Records, Vol. 35, pp. 624–28.
3. Information from Mrs. Beula Burdwell Farley, interviewed by the author, Sanderson, Tex., 1965.
4. Returns from Regular Army Cavalry Regiments, 1833–1916, National Archives, Washington, D.C.
5. Cross Dodd, interviewed by the author, Austin, Tex., 1962.
6. Ibid.
7. Farley interview, 1965.
8. Ibid.
9. Mrs. Rosa Babb Stapp, interviewed by the author, Alpine, Tex., 1965.
10. Judge Roy Bean Visitor Center, original letter on display, Langtry, Tex.
11. Lillie Langtry, *The Days I Knew*, (New York: George H. Doran, 1925), pp. 195–200.
12. Mrs. Myrtle Babb Cash, interviewed by the author, Langtry, Tex., 1965.
13. Forest C. Pogue, *George C. Marshall: Education of a General* (New York: Viking, 1963), pp. 86-88.
14. Guy Skiles, interviewed by the author, Langtry, Tex., 1964.
15. Farley interview, 1965.
16. Dodd interview, 1962.
17. "Who Remembers Charlie Small?" *Frontier Times*, Vol. 22, No. 5, Feb. 1945, pp. 122-23.
18. Harvey Hall, interviewed by the author, Langtry, Tex., 1963.
19. Simon Shaw, Jr., interviewed by the author, Del Rio, Tex., 1964.
20. U.S. Department of State, Consular Reports, 812.00/18119.
21. Guy Skiles interview, 1964.
22. Information from Robert Gatlin, interviewed by the author, Langtry, Tex., c.1985.
23. Ibid.
24. Rufus Kessler, personal communication, August 6, 1980.

INDEX

The author standing on the porch of the abandoned Jersey Lilly saloon in 1937. The sign above him had fallen from its original position on the porch roof and had been tacked to the posts supporting the roof. The building shows the effects of many years of abuse and neglect.

The author in 1996 standing on the porch of the Jersey Lilly Saloon, restored by the Texas Highway Department in 1939. In 1968, the Saloon became part of the Judge Roy Bean Visitor Center. The Center also features a collection of Bean memorabilia and six dioramas with accompanying sound programs depicting some highlights of Judge Roy Bean's life in West Texas, as well as a garden of native flora. (Photo courtesy of Russel Skiles.)